From Discipline to Responsibility:

Principles for Raising Children Today

by

Regenia Mitchum Rawlinson

ISBN 0-932796-79-6

Library of Congress Catalog Card No. 97-60034

Printing (Last Digit)

7   6   5   4   3   2   1

Publisher—

Educational Media Corporation®
P.O. Box 21311
Minneapolis, MN 55421-0311

(612) 781-0088

Production editor—

Don L. Sorenson

Graphic design—

Earl Sorenson

Illustrator—

Maggie McCaskill

Dedication

This book is affectionately dedicated to the family I love, live with, and know best, in gratefulness and love:

David, David II, Bradford,
and Brittany Rawlinson

Additionally, my father died before I was able to finish this book. He and my mother (still living) were tremendous parents. I lovingly dedicate this book to them:

Solomon Mitchum

(deceased October, 1994)

Hazel Mitchum

About the Author

Regenia Mitchum Rawlinson, M.Ed. is guidance director and counselor at Northwestern High School in Rock Hill, South Carolina. An award winning educator, she has 21 years of experience in education as a teacher and counselor. She has worked with a number of programs for "at risk" youths from diverse cultural and economic backgrounds. She has served as a facilitator for a number of parenting groups and has been extended invitations to speak on numerous topics in a variety of settings. Mrs. Rawlinson is married and has three children.

Table of Contents

Introduction

Parents are diverse in their cultural experiences, environmental backgrounds, and social statuses. Consequently, perceptions of what parenting really means may differ from parent to parent. Given these factors, how can one possibly speak on parenting issues to such a diverse group? The school is host to a complex student population. The professionals in education have had to develop a curriculum that would address the needs of each child regardless of his or her background. Attempting to provide each child with an individual curriculum would have been cost prohibitive and difficult to manage and implement. Instead, the educational community generated a list of goals to help students acquire the skills necessary to succeed in life. Some of these goals include: all students will learn how to read, write, and perform mathematical operations, all students will have a career plan before leaving high school, and all students will meet the standards of a proficiency exam. Educators then taught each child according to the goals stated. All children were not taught the same way or necessarily involved in the same coursework, but all worked toward meeting these goals.

Approaching parenting issues based on this model is what we will discuss in this book. Being able to identify principles and then apply them to your particular situation is what makes culture, environment, or social status of little consequence.

Crime is on the rise, teenage pregnancy is very much a sobering reality, and perpetrators of violence are getting younger and younger. A wealth of materials has been written and published in the past years on the topic of raising children, but something is still terribly wrong.

A great deal of the literature outline programs that could be used to address responsibility, discipline, cooperation, communication, self-esteem, and encouragement. A review of these plans offers hope and has some merit, but they often leave parents confused about what is best for their children.

Nevertheless, these critical parenting issues cannot be ignored or treated as trivial. Responsibility, high self-esteem, discipline, encouragement, communication and cooperation all play vital roles in the development of well rounded individuals who are committed to being the best people they were created to be.

The extent to which programs are able to help parents resolve many of the child rearing issues generally depend on training of the parents and the availability of materials.

However, raising children involves much more than programs and materials. It is about bringing children up to be productive, contributing, and responsible members of society. The probability of raising such children is enhanced if parents make decisions about the welfare and needs of their children based on principles and not programs.

As parents you need to consider principles which will be embraced in your family. These principles will have a tremendous impact on the lives of your children for years to come; maybe for as long as they live. It is with this thought in mind and the fact that your grandchildren may be exposed to the same principles which make careful selection of principles critical.

It is the concept of using principles to raise children that is the focus of this book.

Part One:
Discipline

She wondered out loud what had gone wrong, and she hoped someone had some answers for her.

What Is Discipline?

A short time ago I was cornered in the hallway of my guidance department by a frantic and desperate parent. Mrs. Williams had just spent an extremely trying weekend with Shemeka, her teenage daughter. Shemeka stayed out from 7:00 p.m. Friday night

---

until 6:00 a.m. Saturday morning. When she returned home, she refused to tell her parents where she had been and was rude and sassy. At 10:00 p.m. on Saturday night, Mrs. Williams went into Shemeka's room only to find her missing. She called the police to report this thirteen-year-old as a runaway. At 11:00 a.m. on Sunday morning, Shemeka was brought home in a patrol car. The police picked her up as she walked in the downtown area with other teenagers. Although Shemeka protested, on Monday morning Mrs. Williams insisted that she report to school. Frustrated to the point of tears, she now found herself seeking help. Mrs. Williams did not understand Shemeka's rebellious behavior and ungrateful attitude. She wondered out loud what had gone wrong, and she hoped someone had some answers for her.

I invited her into my office where she outlined for me a brief history of how Shemeka was raised. In summary, Shemeka rarely received consequences for breaking the rules of the home or for many other inappropriate behaviors. Expectations were clearly outlined and discussed regularly, but Shemeka met them on a "want to" basis. She was lavished with everything from the latest toy to the most up-to-date clothing. She was allowed to make decisions very early about social activities.

Like Mrs. Williams, you often face discipline problems with your children which are difficult to understand and endure. These issues become particularly stressful when there are no clear cut answers or no simple solutions. The purpose of this section is to examine what discipline is, how to build an atmosphere and relationship where discipline can be effective, and principles to use as guidelines as you seek ways to address discipline problems with your children.

According to *Webster's Dictionary*, discipline is training that produces orderliness, obedience and self-control. This can best be accomplished if five principles—loving, nurturing, training, forewarning, and correcting—are present and working together.

Love

A parent once asked, "When they are yelling and screaming, how do I deal with them in a loving manner?"

The foundation and most important principle of discipline in your relationship with your children is love. If the love bond is strong, the relationship will remain intact when simple or complex issues arise that cause stress in the relationship. Some examples are: disagreements over clothes, choice in friends, choice in boyfriends or girlfriends, eating habits, keeping room clean, completing chores, making good grades in school, behaving in school, alcohol, and sex.

Knowing that these issues will arise, the question then becomes—how will you handle them when they occur? Deciding on the method which is most appropriate for you and your children is a task that should be given serious consideration; but whatever the approach, it needs to be from the standpoint of love.

The question in your mind right now may be—how do I approach every situation from the standpoint of love? This is a concern not only for you but for many parents. A parent once asked, "When they are yelling and screaming, how do I deal with them in a loving manner?" These circumstances are taxing, but they are also opportunities to show your children that they cannot force you to act in unloving ways. Some examples of these unloving ways are: yelling back, screaming just as hard, hitting your children to make them stop, and calling your children names.

In order to interact consistently with your children in loving ways, it is important to remember how you want or wanted your parents to respond to you. For the most part, your children would like to be treated with:

- Patience
- Gentleness
- Respect

- Forgiveness
- Self-control
- Understanding
- Loving authority
- Help
- Care

If you and your children do not have a strong foundation of love, now is the time to start building and strengthening your love bond. This is necessary if you want to be the best parent you can be. In the absence of a strong love bond, your relationship will only endure in the absence of stress.

How can you begin to strengthen love bonds? Strengthening a love bond starts with an examination of how you respond to your children. If you want to develop or maintain a strong bond with them, regularly evaluating how you react and interact with them in a variety of situations is necessary. This can be accomplished by asking yourself questions such as: "Am I responding in loving or unloving ways?" "What kind of message am I sending them?" By doing so, you will be able to monitor and make changes if your action or attitude threatens to weaken or destroy the love bond between you and your children.

You are not perfect—no one is. However, how you respond and interact with your children determines how your children will view you as a parent. If your contact with them is generally positive, they will see you as a parent who loves and cares for them. On the other hand, if your approach to them is negative, they will be unsure of your love and will have questions about how much you value them. This does not mean that you should excuse or accept everything your children do in an effort to keep them happy and free from consequences; on the contrary, it means that you should consistently provide appropriate structure, discipline, and guidance for your children. This is the only way they will grow to be the responsible individuals you want them to be. As a result, your love bond will mature into something beautiful— a cherished relationship!

Nurturing

It is also important that you tell others who love you and your children about your plans of being a nurturing parent.

Hold dear, foster, sustain, appreciate, prize, bring up, rear, value, treasure, and cherish. According to Webster, all of these words describe nurturing as a human experience. In your effort to become a nurturing parent, you must be committed to invest the time, consistency, love, and whatever else is needed to promote a positive relationship.

Jessie's father vowed to spend at least 30 minutes with Jessie daily. His determination to do this was evidenced by the fact that he shared his plans with his closest friend. He wasted no time; he started immediately. The 30 minutes were spent engaging in activities chosen by Jessie. Sometimes they would play games, go for rides, play some type of sport, or just simply talk. When Jessie chose to use this time to talk, he shared many experiences about his school days, friendships, peer pressure, and his interest in girls. Jessie's relationship with his father evolved to an admirable point. Because his father was committed to being a nurturing parent, Jessie felt secure in sharing some deeply personal issues with him. No matter what Jessie told him, he was always willing to listen and to offer guidance and encouragement without judgment.

The significant factor about this story is the time, commitment, and consistency demonstrated by Jessie's father. Jessie's father made a conscious decision to do whatever was necessary to forge a relationship and to be a nurturing parent. You must also do the same if you want this type of relationship with your children. It is also important that you tell others who love you and your children about your plans of being a nurturing parent. Informing others of your intentions will motivate you to maintain your commitment to being the best parent you can be—a nurturing one!

Your children are constantly growing and changing. Consequently, they will need a variety of things at different times and stages of development. But, a nurturing environment is critical.

Creating a nurturing environment can be done in several ways. However, the approach you use to establish such an environment should demonstrate your love for your children. Your children should feel confident that you are developing a nurturing environment because you love them and not because it is something required by societal norms. Whatever method you use, be sure that it is suitable to your situation and that it causes feelings of togetherness for your entire family.

Training

Remember, you can only hold your children accountable for what you have taught them.

Another principle of discipline is training. Training is teaching or instructing children in the things necessary for them to be responsible and productive members of society.

Training takes time, commitment and effort. Sometimes, however, you may spend enormous amounts of time and effort in teaching and instructing your children, but attain only minimal results. There is no guarantee how much your child will learn in a given situation, but you must continue to move forward and with your best efforts. A few suggestions are listed below as you proceed.

- Get your child's attention. Before you instruct, you must have your child's full and undivided attention. Make sure your child can hear you. Make sure your child is looking at you. Make sure that the environment is not noisy or detracting.

- Make your instructions clear, precise and specific.

- The amount and substance of information given should be age and maturity appropriate.

- Break down task into small steps so that your child can perform each one well.

- Provide praise or other rewards when your child performs each step.

- Make clear what standards are going to be used for evaluating performance.

- Work with your child to solve any problems that arise in the course of completing a task.

- Tell your child what was done correctly and incorrectly so your child will know what was done right or what needs to be improved.

A child needs to learn everything. John Locke suggested that children are born with a clean slate, having no knowledge at all. Therefore, it is the responsibility of the parent to teach them. Below is listed a few of the things children need to be taught. Please add to the list on the lines provided.

- How to be responsible.

- How to share.

- How to love.

- How to be respectful.

- How to be kind.

- How to manage money.

- How to be honest.

- How to be trustworthy.

- How to take a bath.

- How to hold a spoon.

- How to walk.

- How to dress.

- How to tie shoes.

- How to brush teeth.

- How to play.

- How to work.
- How to be cooperative.
- How to be helpful.
- _____
- _____
- _____
- _____
- _____

Remember, you can only hold your children accountable for what you have taught them. It never ceases to amaze me, when parents scold their children, they usually say something like, "You should have known better." My question always is, "Did you tell them better?" Do not assume your children know even the simplest things if you have not personally taught them yourself. Even in the case of school work, you should periodically check on the progress of your children to make sure they are learning the concepts and facts they need to know. In other words, you either teach your children or make certain that they are being taught. In the end, it is your responsibility to see to it that your children are given an opportunity to learn all they need to know.

In addition to verbally instructing your children, modeling is another powerful and effective tool in training your children how and what to do. Children generally will learn and retain more if it is modeled for them.

Through modeling, children will have a clear understanding of your expectations. For example, if you want your children to be truthful, you have to be honest at all times. For instance, when someone calls and you really do not want to talk, you should not say, "I'm cooking right now—I'll call you back," if that is not the truth. Children model actions that they are exposed to; they do not discriminate between those that are appropriate and those that are not.

You must be conscious of everything you say or do in the presence of your children. Remember, words + modeling = teaching.

Forewarning

When you forewarn your children, you are giving them gentle and friendly reproof as well as counseling or warning against fault or oversight. In other words, you remind them that your expectations are not being met and that they need to get back on track. You give them a chance to get it right.

How you remind them is very important. Reminding them in ways that cause shame, feelings of worthlessness, guilt, rebellion, low self-esteem, and bewilderment, only creates tension. Statements such as, "You are lazy," "You can't do anything right," "You are stupid," "You are a liar," "You can't understand anything," and "You never do what I ask you" can cause so much damage to the relationship that it would be difficult to repair.

Talking with your children in ways that are not judgmental, blaming, or challenging helps to eliminate rebellious responses, enhances the relationship with your children, and opens communication lines.

Speaking with your children in a calm and caring fashion is not always easy. However, focusing on the goal of eliminating or changing behavior, rather than concentrating on trying to remake your children, is more productive and will lessen stress. When your attention is centered on the behavior, the need to lash out or attack your children's worth decreases. This will enhance your children's willingness to listen to what you have to say. Therefore, your children will hear you out because they trust you to protect them from "Verbal Battering."

Parents would like to believe that they have the power to change their children and make them into what they want them to be. Fortunately, this is not the case. If we had that kind of control over children, they may not grow and develop into the unique persons they were born to be. We, however, do have an obligation to forewarn them when their behavior is inappropriate and unacceptable. We also must provide correction if children refuse to bring their behavior in line with the standards or principles that govern the family.

Correction

> *The principles of love, teaching, nurturing, and fore-*
> *warning should be factors undergirding any corrective*
> *action taken by you.*

The last principle of discipline is that of correction. It is important to remember what the purpose of correction is: to help the child develop and grow in all areas—socially, emotionally, physically, and spiritually. The goal is not for you to release your anger.

Correction should take place in the context of love. It should be administered in a calm and caring fashion. It is better to wait until you can correct your children without the possibility of physical or emotional abuse, than to act in a way that will cause you and your children undue stress or pain.

There are many ways in which you can correct your children. When you are trying to figure out what kind of correction to use, ask yourself these questions:

- Will this damage the child emotionally or physically? When I speak of damage, I do not mean hurt. Often correction does hurt—there is no way around that. What I do mean is—will it leave bruises in the emotions or on the body?

- Am I calm enough to figure out the appropriate correction? Does the correction relate directly to the problem? If a child spills milk, giving the child a cloth and instructing the child to clean it up is an appropriate way to handle it. After a few times of this, milk spilling will diminish.

- Will this help the child to be more responsible?

- Will this attack and weaken the child's self-esteem?

- Can this be done with respect and dignity?

- Have I given this enough thought?

- Will this help the child make better decisions in the future?

There are many different programs which suggest types and systems of correcting problems which parents might experience with their children. Nonetheless, you need to exercise caution when using such programs. Programs are usually written in a step by step design. Success with such an approach requires the ability or willingness to follow the steps to the letter. Addressing difficulties according to fundamental principles allow for flexibility and is naturally more effective. Principles provide foundational truths on which to build—programs give pat answers. Principles are what you believe and how you live—programs are what someone else believe. Principles are a way of life—programs are a way for the day. Principles provide a guide and help you to apply techniques that are specific to the individual needs of children. Program are formulated and do not allow for personal differences among children. The principles of love, teaching, nurturing, and forewarning should be the factors undergirding any corrective action taken by you.

When problems arise, you will have to decide how to respond. You can: do nothing, provide parental consequences, allow natural consequences to address the issue, or use abusive or vindictive correction. We will examine these approaches to determine how and when each is most effective.

Doing Nothing

When you decide to do nothing, you are essentially giving your children permission to deal with the problem in any way they see fit. This may also lead the children to believe there is no problem with which to deal. It would be wonderful if children had enough experience to know what to do—but they don't—that's why they need you.

Sometimes the only intervention necessary is pointing out alternatives or talking with your children. To do nothing is to give children a license to do what they want, when they want, and how they want to do it.

Children need your guidance and correction as they strive to develop and grow to their fullest potential in every area.

Consequences

The severity of the consequences is not nearly as important as the consistent administration of them.

There are two kinds of consequences—natural and parental. Natural consequences occur as a result of poor decisions made on the part of the child. Parental consequences occur when you decide on the kind of correction necessary to eliminate unacceptable behavior.

To better understand these two concepts, we will discuss each separately.

Natural Consequences. Your child touched a hot stove—what should you do? Give what is needed—medical attention, support and love. Yelling or telling the child, "I told you not to touch that stove" serves no useful purpose. By now the child knows that this was a poor choice and has learned a lesson that will not soon be forgotten. The child made a "D" on a major spelling exam for which there was no preparation. The child's decision not to study resulted in a final grade of "C" in a class where an "A" had previously been earned. What do you do? Allow the natural consequence of getting a "C" for a final grade to stand. Do not call the teacher and beg her to give your child another chance to take the test. Even if your child wants to do this—do not encourage or allow it. If you do this or permit it, your child will assume that you will always back him or her up when a poor decision is made. You should not listen to moaning and groaning about the test being too hard or the teacher being mean and unfair; these are excuses that keep your child from accepting responsibility for his or her own actions.

Allowing children to experience the natural consequences of poor decisions will help them to be more responsible. A responsible child is an encouraged child. This does not mean that you withhold guidance, parental consequences, or suggestions about how to avoid the same thing in the future. It only suggests that you do not interfere with your children having the opportunity to learn from mistakes.

Your question might be—How do I know when natural consequences are appropriate for the behavior? There are no exact or pat answers. You have to make the final determination based on your individual situation. However, I have found these questions helpful in determining whether natural consequences are appropriate and sufficient.

- Is this the first time this has occurred?

- Have we talked about parental consequences if this behavior occurs again?

- Does the child know my feelings about this behavior?

- Is this serious enough for parental consequences, even if this is the first time?

- Is the natural consequence dangerous and/or life threatening, such as a young child playing near a swimming pool? The natural consequence may be death. You certainly do not want that.

- Will the natural consequence occur too far in the future to be effective?

If you answered "no" to the first three questions, then a natural consequence could be appropriate. However, if you answered "yes" to the last three questions, parental intervention is needed.

If you decide that a natural consequence is appropriate, it is wise at this time to discuss and decide on a parental consequence if this occurs again. The child should know what your expectations are for future behavior and performance.

Parental Consequences. Your child has left toys in the middle of the floor. You have asked your child several times to put the toys away after playing. So far nothing has worked. Parental consequences in this situation is definitely in order.

Parental consequences as often as possible, should be given according to a planned course of action. They do not have to be, but it lessens confusion and rebellion if they are. You, as well as the child, need to know exactly what will happen if a certain behavior continues. For example, you tell your child that the next time the toys are not put away after playing, you will take and keep any toys left in the middle of the floor.

Bobby has taken a cookie from the pantry just fifteen minutes before dinner. Mother has never told him that she did not want him to do this. In fact, he has done this several times and no objections were raised by Mother. But this time Mother sees him and says, "Put it back and go to your room. It's almost dinner time. You know you shouldn't have a cookie!" Bobby responds with tears and anger—"I got one yesterday." "You didn't say anything then." "It's not fair."

Bobby felt Mother was unfair because she never told him how she felt about eating a cookie before dinner. In other words, Mother decided that having a cookie before dinner was no longer permitted. The problem occurred when she did not inform Bobby of her decision.

You have the right to change or adjust limits and rules. That is not the issue here. The difficulty occurred when Mother gave Bobby no prior warning that there was going to be a change. Bobby reacted with anger and rebellion because he viewed Mother's action as arbitrary and unjustified. This is what we call "Vindictive Correction." We will talk about this in more detail later.

What needed to happen for Mother to be fair? It was necessary for Mother to talk with Bobby about the issue, explaining her expectations and outlining what the consequences would be if he continued. Bobby could then be held accountable for future actions because he would be aware of the consequences before he made his decision.

Parental consequences are most effective when you do several things. First, a discussion with your children about your expectations is the foundation upon which the idea of parental consequences is built. Your children must know what you expect before they can follow through.

Secondly, your children need to be able to meet your expectations without too much difficulty. If they are too high or unreasonable for your children's age and level of maturity, your children will certainly fail. If your children have too many negative experiences, they will become discouraged and self-esteem will suffer. You want your children to be successful, so be reasonable and realistic!

Thirdly, after your children fully understand what your expectations are, they need to be told specifically what will happen if they fail to adhere to them. Make them aware of the parental consequences for each behavior. At a minimum, your children need to understand that something will happen if they decide to ignore what you outline for them.

Here are some things to consider when you are trying to decide on consequences:

- Consequences should be something that can be administered immediately; with each passing minute they lose their effectiveness.

- Consequences should be something that you are *willing* and *able* to enforce.

- Consequences should be free of abusive or vindictive corrections.

- Consequences should be pertinent to the inappropriate behavior.

- Consequences should be given consistently; if they are not, the likelihood of the behavior occurring again dramatically increases and becomes harder to eliminate in the future.

A very crucial point to remember is that the severity of the consequences is not nearly as important as the consistent administration of them.

Now that you have your plan of action—accept no excuses. Children are full of them. You are smart; you know your children well enough to know when they are trying to avoid responsibility for their decisions.

Be consistent. If your child leaves toys in the middle of the floor three times and you take them away, but the fourth time you fail to do so—you have blown it. You have to start all over again.

Remember, it is not how harsh or severe the consequences are, it is how consistent they are administered that's makes the difference.

Action speaks louder than words! Once you have discussed your expectations and explained the consequences, act if the child gets out of line. Administer the consequences calmly and firmly without further discussion.

Keshia was told that she would lose the privilege of riding her bike for two days if she rode into the streets again. One day as her mother was cleaning and preparing for guests, she looked out of the window and saw Keshia in the middle of the street. She called Keshia, told her to put her bike away and informed her that she could not ride it for two days. Keshia promised her mother that she would not do it again and begged for another chance. Her mother reminded her of their discussion and repeated the consequence. Her mother resisted the temptation of lecturing Keshia about the ills of disobedience and from pointing the "I told you so finger." Instead she calmly and firmly administered the consequence.

Be aware that children will not go down without a fight. If they have become accustomed to doing things one way, and all of a sudden you want to change that, they are not going to like it. They have to find out if you really mean it, so expect testing. Children may pick up their clothes the first or second time after you have a discussion with them about keeping their clothes off the floor, but you may walk into their room one day and see nothing but clothes all over the place. When you remind them of the consequences, you may hear, "I was going to do it." "You didn't give me a chance." "You didn't give me time." "I was hanging them up." "You are mean." "I hate you." Remember, they want to fight with you. Do not give them what they want. Remain calm and be consistent.

It is of vital importance that you only give choices and outline consequences that you know you will be able to live with. If you do not think that you can take the toys away, do not say you will! Use something that you know you can stick with. Mean what you say, say what you mean, and do what you say!

Abusive or Vindictive Correction

This kind of correction does not have love as it's basis and the purpose of it is not teaching. Rather, it is used as a means of hurting or getting back at the child in some way and usually occurs in the absence of clearly defined limits or inconsistent enforcement of limits. Abusive or vindictive correction is characterized by abusive language, physical harm, and attacks on the child's self worth.

When abusive or vindictive correction is used by you, your children may become confused and unsure about your love for them. This state of confusion and uncertainty frequently causes fear. You want your children to respect you—not fear you. Fear produces discouraged children, irresponsibility, and poor decision making. This happens because fear cannot live in conjunction with reason and thought. They are enemies, and enemies do not work together.

It is far better for you to set up some parental consequences than to use this kind of correction as a way of getting children to cooperate, follow directions, or obey. This kind of correction can be summed up in one word—destructive!

Part Two:
Cooperation

Just like you can't make a car run on three wheels, even big, powerful adults cannot make small children do something that they have absolutely make up their mind that they do not want to do.

What is Cooperation?

Jan opened the door of the white medicine cabinet mounted on the wall of her bathroom. She grabbed a clear plastic medicine spoon and headed for the kitchen. She carefully sterilized the spoon in hot water and allowed it to cool. She opened the refrigerator where she had stored the antibiotics prescribed by the doctor just an hour earlier for her son's ear infection. She poured the dosage instructed by the doctor, one teaspoon, into the medicine spoon. She called her two-year-old son to her.

When he arrived at her feet, she picked him up and said, "You will feel better after you take this. Come on sweetie." Willingly the child opened his mouth. She slowly tilted the spoon in an effort to dispense the antibiotics. The contents of the spoon gradually reached his mouth. The initial taste of it brought an unexpected and messy reaction. Before she knew what hit her, she was sprayed with pink antibiotics in her face and her clothing needed to be dry cleaned. In desperation, she called for reinforcement—her husband. Dad confidently took his son and the refilled medicine spoon. Holding his son securely in his arms, he demanded that the child take the medication. Yelling, screaming, and with many tears, his son answered, "No! No! No!" After several attempts, Dad gave up. The spoon yielded to the child's juice in his favorite cup mixed with the proper dosage of his medication. Needless to say, the parents were relieved that this worked.

This story illustrates the fact that even big powerful adults cannot make a small child do something that he has absolutely made up his mind that he does not want to do. All human beings, big or small, are born with a will. Sometimes the "small will" does not want to yield to the "big will." As true as this is, a child will learn to do what you ask him to do, in most cases, if an environment of unconditional love is instituted very early. Consequently, securing a child's cooperation would be less troublesome.

Unconditional love involves principles that can help you understand your children and respond to them with new and refreshing insights. When you can interact with your children in this manner, cooperation will follow.

Cooperation is not asking your children's permission for you to be the boss or the parent; it is not about negotiating. It is about getting children to do what you want them to do in a manner that meets your expectations and standards. You may choose to modify the consequences, but it is a mistake to compromise your standards and expectations.

Many people would call this obedience. So be it. What is wrong with this word? As long as children understand that you are the one who makes the rules and they are expected to abide by them, why fight over words?

I have found that it is not the rules or standards that present the greatest difficulty. No matter how lenient rules and standards are, children will find some way of declaring that they are not fair. The problem is to get children to abide by them willingly or at least without excessive debate.

It is crucial, however, for you never to lose sight of the fact that cooperation will never become reality in a hostile and uncaring environment. You need to provide an atmosphere of patience, love, care, and safety. The children must feel that you are there for them no matter what. They need to know that even when they fall short of your expectations—they still are loved.

When children know that you care for them, the desire to cooperate will follow. Getting children to cooperate is not a quick fix program. It is not a magical formula. It is not a chart that displays stars for cooperative behavior. It is a way of life!

Motivating children to cooperate involves principles. If these principles are not applied to your daily life, you will, without a doubt, lose many opportunities to foster cooperation in your children.

Children do not automatically know what behavior is cooperative and uncooperative. They depend on you to show them. Uncooperative children cry out for models that can show them how to act more appropriately. As smart as children are, they still learn and retain more by observing the behavior of others. That is why it is necessary for you to live what you teach. It is unrealistic to believe that children will do what you say instead of what they see you do. Remember, **WORDS + MODELING = TEACHING!**

Understanding

One principle of unconditional love is understanding. To understand someone is to have some insight in to how that person responds and sees oneself in relation to the world, in relation to oneself, and in relation to others.

It is not always easy to grasp what another person is trying to communicate to you. However, observing actions, attitudes, and words could give some valuable information.

Once you have an idea of what your children are saying to you, you have a better chance of responding and interacting appropriately and effectively with them.

List four of your child's likes:

1. _____

2. _____

3. _____

4. _____

List four of your child's dislikes:

1. _____

2. _____

3. _____

4. _____

List one thing your child gets excited about:

_____

What is your child's favorite color:

_____

These are just a few to get you thinking. Continue to observe your children daily to get a clearer understanding of who they are.

Educational Media Corporation®

Non-Judgmental Posture

When children feel they personally are judged or attacked rather than the inappropriate behavior, they will do everything in their power to avoid appearing anything less than perfect in your eyes. Children may also react to a judgmental posture by being rebellious and unruly.

When children have these feelings of worthlessness, they often resort to fabricating, covering up, or lying. When children get to this point, they spend a lot of time feeling worthless, unappreciated, and rejected.

There are times when you need to call mistakes to your children's attention. You would be less than a responsible parent if you failed to do so. When these occasions arise, they need to be handled using helpful language and demeanor. Here are a few suggestions:

- Be warm and supportive.

- Remain calm.

- Be patient.

- Talk only about the specific behavior—not the child.

- Discuss ways of avoiding the same mistakes next time.

- Use words that build and not tear down.

The use of the words and phrases such as should ("You should have known better") ought ("You ought to have done it this way"), must ("You must have known that this would not work"), never ("You never do anything right"), and always ("You always say things like that") imply judgment and is very destructive to a child's feeling of self-worth.

Consequences

Sometimes it is necessary to chastise a child because of a decision the child has made. For instance, you have told your children that they are not allowed to play in the street. You come back home early one day and discover them pitching ball in the middle of the street. What should you do? Should you impose a parental consequence or allow a natural consequence to occur? Read the section on discipline for a full explanation of natural and parental consequences.

There are many options available to you that can be used to teach. Isn't that the whole point of consequences—to teach? If you do not agree with this point of view, you need to ask yourself why you do what you do.

Remember, consequences can be powerful teaching tools if: 1) used fairly, 2) done in the context of love, 3) used for the purpose of teaching 4) promotes good decision making, and 5) encourages responsibility.

Oversee Physical, Emotional, Social, Academic, and Spiritual Development

As a parent you are charged with the responsibility of seeing that your child develops and grows in every area—physical, emotional, academic, and spiritual.

You do not owe your children the fulfillment of every want and desire, but you are commanded by God to provide them with the things that will help them to mature and become responsible adults.

List one thing that you can do to oversee each area of your child's development:

Physical:

Social:

Academic:

Spiritual:

Nurture Them

You have the responsibility to make certain that your children have everything they need to develop and grow to their fullest potential. One way you can achieve this is by nurturing, supplying the children with all that is needed when it is needed.

As children grow, they need different things at different times in their lives. As infants, they will need complete care from you. When they enter school, they need materials, time, and support. When they are in high school, they need guidance on course selections, advice about friends, support, and lots of encouragement.

Your children will change many times, and their needs will change, too. However, the one thing that all children need is love; no matter how old or how young they are. Love is what makes nurturing real and possible. Without it, you are not able to come close to giving your children what they need at any point in their lives.

Discipline

Discipline is training that leads to orderliness, obedience and self-control. These three products of discipline are what you need to remember as you decide how to discipline your children.

Orderliness is a necessary ingredient of the society in which we live. Without it, chaos would be the norm. In the same light, a lack of order in the home produces an environment that is in constant turmoil.

In these so called enlightened times, child rearing experts like to stay clear of the word *obedience.* They like to use less threatening words like *compromise* and *negotiate.* These terms are soothing, but fall short of addressing how children are to respond to parents. God commands that children obey their parents, and when parents accept less, children suffer for it. When children are allowed to disobey, confusion and rebellion result.

A rebellious attitude can lead to a lack of self-control. Children are often out of control because somewhere at some point in their lives, adults allowed them to do what they wanted to do, when they wanted to do it, and how they wanted to do it.

Teaching children self-control has to start early. When you give in to the demands of children because they throw temper tantrums, they quickly learn that this kind of behavior will get them what they want. Consequently, they are less likely to develop self-control.

You also need to be constantly aware that children model what they see. An out of control parent, often produces an out of control child. You must exercise self-control in everything you do.

Disciplining children is not a program or a quick fix—it is a way of life and should always be done in the context of love and should be an integral part of your plans to encourage cooperation from your child.

Individual Differences

From what we know of human beings and their characteristics, each person is unique. Even identical twins are unique. Being aware of this, as a parent, adds to your understanding of why your first child is nothing like your second.

Comparing children is very destructive and useless. It would be helpful for you to figure out and work with each individual child in ways that acknowledge and encourage their uniqueness.

List the names of your children and at least three things about each that is different and unique. List two things that you can do to acknowledge their differences in a positive way.

Name

_____

Three unique and different characteristics

1. _____
2. _____
3. _____

How I can acknowledge those differences

1. _____
2. _____
3. _____

Name

_____

Three unique and different things

1. _____
2. _____
3. _____

How I can acknowledge those differences.

1. _____
2. _____
3. _____
4. _____

Educational Media Corporation®

Teach

Words + modeling = teaching

You need to diligently teach your children all things that are required to live a successful and responsible life.

Your question may be, what are some things that need to be taught? This can be addressed in specific terms or general ones. It is important to look at both. However, in this section, we will look at the general terms.

Below you will find some general areas that should be taught. These are not all inclusive and you should seek to add to this list as you acquire more information.

- Social skills.
- Responsibility.
- Cooperation.
- Sharing.
- Good moral values.
- Honesty.
- The value of an education.
- Good decision making skills.
- The importance of identifying and using gifts and talents.
- Respect.
- Courtesy.

Remember, children learn by example and words. Our behaviors are powerful teaching tools; good or bad, our children learn from them. Keep this formula in mind: **words + modeling = teaching.**

Invite

Everything we say and do has a way of inviting or rejecting another person. The words we use, the tone of our voice, the way we talk, and the way we look at another person, all send a message. That message is received and interpreted as one of invitation or one of indifference.

It does not take a genius to figure out that children will respond favorably to adults who send the message of invitation.

Remember, words can build or they can tear down any relationship. Words help heal or they can cause pain. Words can be pleasant or words can be harsh. Words can express warmth or words can express anger and resentment. The famous childhood saying "Sticks and stones may break my bones but words will never hurt me," is false. Words may not be able to break your bones, but words can cause deep emotional scars which may last for a lifetime. Never underestimate the power of words.

You must understand that what you say, how you say it (tone of voice), and body posture must all send the same message if you want your children to see them as inviting.

Observe

Observing your children will give you more insight into who they are better than anything I can suggest. Watching your children in the park, at restaurants, at home, in the yard, sleeping, interacting with peers, and in other situations will yield vast amounts of information. This knowledge can assist you in determining and understanding your child's unique qualities, likes, and dislikes.

List other places that you can observe your children:

_____

_____

_____

_____

List activities that you can observe your children doing:

_____

_____

_____

_____

Never Give Up

I worked with a family once that was having some severe problems with one of their children. We will call her Kim. Kim's mother came in to speak with me about the difficulties. She was at the end of her rope. She had tried everything. Nothing worked. After talking with Kim's mother for an hour, her last statements were, "I give up." "I don't know what to do any more." "I cannot give Kim what she needs and I'm not willing to keep trying." I thought how hopeless this mother sounded. I, perhaps, would not have felt such a deep sense of loss if the child was more than eight years old.

When you are experiencing difficult times with your children—hold on. One thing for sure, nothing remains the same; there will be a change. You can influence the outcome by not losing faith and by communicating to your children that despite the adversity; you still have hope.

It is important that your children know that your commitment is strong and that you are there for them.

Acknowledge

It is very important that your child feels acknowledged for just being who he or she is and a member of the human race. Small things like a smile, a hug, or a kiss work wonders! Little acts such as these will reassure your child of your love. Practice acts of random kindness and reassurance with your child.

List ten ways that you can acknowledge your child:

1. _____

2. _____

3. _____

4. _____

5. _____

6. _____

7. _____

8. _____

9. _____

10. _____

Long Suffering

The use of this principle in dealing with children is very powerful and absolutely necessary. If you are going to help children grow and mature into responsible adults, you must exercise patience.

Children are going to make mistakes—that is a given. How you react and deal with these errors make the difference. When mistakes are made by children, remember that if they were perfect, they would not need you. That is the whole point—they are not without flaws and they need your help when they are having difficulties.

It is easy for you to become frustrated if a child is whining and complaining. It is very tempting to fuss and use abusive language with your children when they are not moving fast enough for you. Holding back your wrath is difficult when you assign chores and they are not done appropriately or on time.

These everyday routine situations are the ones you have to contend with most often. Whether it is dealing with mistakes or ordinary daily matters, the following may be helpful in managing them successfully:

- Remain calm.

- If you cannot remain calm, remove yourself from the situation until you are able to do so.

- Listen to what the child has to say.

- Use words and body language that will preserve the child's dignity and feeling of self-worth. Let the child know that while you disapprove of the behavior, you still accept and love him or her.

Listen to Your Children

* *
Listening is not something that you can do automatically.
* *

In this busy, hurry-up, both parent working society, listening has become a rare and precious commodity. You must strenuously guard against this becoming true for you and your children.

Take time to listen to your children. This is easier said than done. However, if you want to remain a participant in the lives of your children, you must be willing to spend time with them. This time will provide an opportunity for input, a chance to influence behavior and attitudes, an opportunity to provide guidance, and a chance to learn something about your child.

Listening is not something that you can do automatically. You must conscientiously focus your attention on the person.

Open and Honest

Children are very keen and have a unique sense of when you are not being sincere and honest. Children should be able to depend on you to be as open and honest as age and maturity will allow.

Having a relationship based on these principles will foster trust in children.

If children ask you a direct question give them a direct answer. Sugar coating it or making it sound good does a lot for you, but it only confuses the child if you are not completely truthful with your answers. The child may accept what you say at the time, but will continue to observe to determine if what you said was the truth. The child will also learn that he or she cannot depend on you for sincere and straightforward answers.

Sometimes it is hard for you to be honest with your children—particularly if you believe that a truthful answer will make you look small in your child's eyes. This is understandable but self defeating. Children, for the most part, are very empathic toward others—especially their parents.

You will not lose your place of high esteem with your children if you are open and honest with them, but you will if you are not!

Vulnerability

Children need to know that you are human too. They need to understand that you require love, have feelings, are not perfect, do not know everything, and are capable of making mistakes.

Encourage

The last principle of unconditional love is encouragement. Encouraging children is essential in helping them become what they were created to be. A lack of encouragement will cause children to feel hopeless and helpless.

If you want your children to be successful, you must make every effort to encourage them in the things in which they show interest, talent, and/or possess a special gift in.

Discouragers and Communication Stoppers!

Without good communication between you and your child, cooperation cannot thrive.

I was raised in a family of sixteen brothers and sisters, and loving, dedicated, and committed parents. The competition for attention and time in such a large family was fierce. This atmosphere often gave rise to arguments among my siblings. This was sibling rivalry at it's best. Needless to say, communication (real communication, someone talks and someone listens) suffered. We learned to talk loudly so that people would listen . We certainly did not embrace the E.F. Hutton slogan, "When E.F. Hutton talks, everyone listens." While the other person was speaking, you really did not listen. You aggressively searched the computer banks of your mind to figure out what to say next to ensure that you emerged as the winner of the present verbal confrontation.

It was not until I grew to a very ripe age that I realized I had little skills in communication. I had a difficult time emphasizing and listening for feelings behind words. I am much better now, but I work constantly to improve my communication skills.

You, as a parent, must do the same. Without good communication between you and your child, cooperation cannot thrive. Just as there are behaviors that will encourage children to cooperate and communicate with you, there are also those that will discourage cooperation and, thereby, interfere with communication. Some behaviors to watch out for are: **Questions! Questions! Questions!**

There is a time and a place to ask reasonable questions of your child. However, too many of them will cause the child to clam up rather than open up.

When you want to find out information from your child, ask open ended questions. For example if you wanted to know what your child did in school for a day, asking your child something like "What did you do in school today?" will get a limited response. The answer will most likely be "Nothing." On the other hand if you asked, "What were three things you did in school today?" you will probably get an itemized list. By asking in this manner, you learn what kind of day your child had in school.

Just remember these formulas—Too many questions = closed lips and irritation. Wrong kinds of questions = limited answers, closed lips, and irritation.

I have just the answer! Children should be provided with guidance. However, this does not always mean that you give the answer. There are times when the answer is solicited, needed, or welcomed by your children, but it is essential that children, as much as possible, be given an opportunity to choose appropriate solutions.

Children benefit much more if you listen to them and discuss options for handling situations. Teaching children to consider all possible alternatives and choosing the best solution will help them become effective problem solvers as adults.

I have a grand idea! Using sweet words or distracting the child will only make the child think that what he or she says is not worth listening to.

Deal with what the child is saying to you. Do not suggest doing something to help your child relax or use words designed to get his or her mind off the issue at hand.

Shoulds, oughts, musts. "You should have made an 'A' on this math test." "You ought to have drawn this picture better." "You must be like your brother if you are going to be somebody." Responding to your children in this manner often make them feel inadequate and, in many cases, worthless.

Avoid using these words. If you do not, these words have the power to weaken or destroy your child's self-esteem.

Complete control. You must always maintain a certain degree of control in order to be a powerful influence in the lives of your children. This, however, does not necessarily mean commanding every step, swaying every thought, and directing every action.

When you behave like you are a boot camp sergeant, children have a tendency to be completely rebellious. Sometimes being in control means allowing children to choose.

Know it all! Children must feel that their suggestions are welcomed and will be used if possible. When they begin to feel that they cannot contribute, they will share less and less.

Making jokes and funny remarks. Anything a child shares with you should be taken seriously. When you make jokes or funny remarks, it discourages the child from talking with you about things in the future.

Part Three:
Self-Esteem

If a person does not see himself or herself as worthwhile, lovable, and capable, the chances of that person reaching his or her full potential are limited.

What Is Self-Esteem?

'"I feel so small."—*High school student*

"I can't do anything right."—*Elementary school student*

"Nobody likes me."—*Middle school student*

Comments like these can be heard daily in many different places and in a variety of cultures. No matter where people come from or who they are, the need to be loved and accepted is real. Location, size, nor age make a difference. When people view themselves as losers, worthless, unacceptable, undeserving, or unlovable, statements like these are what you can expect to hear. But what can be done to improve or enhance a person's belief about oneself? In other words, what can be done to enhance self-esteem?

Self-esteem has been the focal point of numerous books and many articles in recent years. The vast majority discuss the need to develop high self-esteem and how to do it.

Most of the literature supports the idea that high self-esteem is important to the development of a healthy personality. I, too, believe it is essential. If a person does not see himself or herself as worthwhile, lovable, and capable, the chances of that person reaching his or her full potential are limited.

The variety of suggestions found in the literature about how to help children develop high self-esteem are many. They cover everything from giving stickers for appropriate behavior to allowing the child to have more responsibility.

All of these suggestions have some merit but may leave you confused about what is best for your children. This confusion may frustrate you to the point it renders you ineffective or actionless.

In order to know how to improve self-esteem, you must know what it means. Professionals define self-esteem as a feeling, a personal evaluation of how much you are worth and how important you are. This evaluation indicates the degree to which you believe in your capabilities, importance, and ability to be successful.

The following stories illustrate this point clearly.

Derek was surrounded by many people who loved and adored him. His mother, grandmother, uncle, father, and two older sisters made it a point to say something encouraging to him daily. They would tell him how smart, creative, handsome, athletic, and likable he was.

There is no doubt that by the time Derek becomes a senior in high school, he will have accomplished his goal of being valedictorian of his class of 346. After graduation, he plans to enter college to study medicine.

On the other hand, there is Johnny. Johnny lives with his mother, grandmother, uncle, father, and two older sisters. Though both families have the same number and category of people, his experiences and interaction with them are markedly different from Derek's.

They often tell Johnny how dumb, ugly, stupid, and uncreative he is. Encouraging words and phrases seldom are heard around his house. Even when he does something that he is proud of, it is ignored or he is asked why he did not do better.

Johnny is failing in school, although he scored in the 90s on his aptitude test. He also has had many referrals to the principal's office for behavior problems.

No one understands why Johnny is having such a difficult time academically and socially. According to his test scores, he should be making A's. He is handsome with beautiful brown eyes. He can throw a baseball incredibly fast and he plays other sports well.

When Johnny was seven, he often talked about being a doctor. Now at fourteen, it is never mentioned by him.

If Johnny's feelings of unworthiness do not change, the likelihood of him realizing his dreams will be greatly diminished.

Exactly when these two boys developed their self-esteem is uncertain, but the stories of Derek and Johnny reminds us that how children feel about themselves has a significant impact on how well they will function in productive ways and utilize their abilities and talents to the fullest.

In order to help children build high self-esteem, you must begin to ask the relevant questions of how this is done and why some children have low self-esteem.

How Do We Come By Our Self-Esteem?

We are not born with either high or low self-esteem. As we grow and interact with people and our environment, self-esteem begins to take shape.

If our experiences with the environment and our contact with people are primarily positive, then we will learn to think of ourselves in positive and acceptable ways.

On the other hand, low self-esteem comes about as a result of largely unsuccessful experiences with the environment and social interaction. Individuals with low self-esteem learn to see themselves as failures and act accordingly.

Therefore, with these things in mind, you must seek to create safe, healthy, loving, caring, supportive, and non-judgmental environments. These kinds of living conditions will enhance and ensure high self-esteem.

How such environments are created must be an individual decision. No one is able to tell you exactly what fits into your particular situation. However, strategies and techniques will have a better chance of enhancing self-esteem if they are built upon the principles of providing children with successful experiences and an environment rich in positive growth opportunities.

Why Is Self-Esteem So Important?

Studies have shown that children with high self-esteem perform better in school. Studies further indicate that children with superior intelligence but low self-esteem may perform poorly in school. Conversely, children with average intelligence but high self-esteem, are likely to be successful.

Children with low self-esteem do not get much enjoyment out of school work or life in general. Often, they have met with failure so many times that school work becomes a threat to further weaken an already low opinion of their ability to succeed. My experiences with children confirm what studies have shown.

In addition, the child is easily distracted due to anxieties about relationships and being accepted by others. These may become even more pronounced during adolescence when peers and body image are the most important.

Children with high self-esteem exhibit confidence in most tasks undertaken. They feel good about their ability to achieve. When the task is a new one, they may have questions or reservations but are able to draw on previous successes to help them overcome feelings of stress. Having this mindset, they are able to be productive and creative in a variety of settings.

High self-esteem is essential if children are going to be creative, be productive, make good decisions, be responsible, and have good wholesome relationships with others.

Indicators of High and Low Self-Esteem

Self-esteem is not constant; it maybe high one day and low the next. Therefore, one incident or one behavior is not a clear indication of a child's level of self-esteem.

When trying to determine the level of self-esteem, looking at the overall characteristics and patterns of behavior are important. For example, a child with high self-esteem will do well in school, relationships, making decisions, and is generally happy. The key is, how does the child perform most of the time?

As you examine the indicators of high and low self-esteem listed below, remember that there may be others which your children exhibit that are not included. As you seek to identify these, please remember that high and low self-esteem, in most cases, can be determined by the manner in which they behave, the words they use when describing themselves in general conversation, interaction with others, and the environment, and their approaches to problem solving.

Over time, for the most part, children with high self-esteem will:

- Be proud, not boastful, of accomplishments.
- Take on responsibility.
- Be honest about feelings.
- Accept new challenges with enthusiasm.
- Have a frustration level that is higher than most children.
- Be helpful.
- Have a positive attitude about self, others, and life.
- Make good decisions.
- Not blame others for mistakes.
- Be able to admit mistakes.
- Not be easily influenced by others.
- Have confidence in abilities.
- Ask for help.

Children with low self-esteem will:

- Avoid situations that provide challenges.

- Talk poorly about self, others, and life.

- Blame others for most things.

- Be unable to admit mistakes.

- Make poor decisions.

- Be easily influenced by others.

- Be defensive.

- Be easily frustrated.

- Have a hard time listing accomplishments.

- Not be proud of accomplishments.

- Look for excuses.

- Lack confidence in abilities.

- Mask true feelings.

To determine the level of your child's self-esteem, a great deal of time needs to be spent in observing and evaluating your child in many environments and under different types of circumstances.

Under What Environmental Conditions Does Positive Self-Esteem Occur?

Creating environmental conditions under which positive self-esteem occurs is similar to planting a garden. The gardener must first decide what is needed for a particular crop. From my experience on a farm, the farmer will need at least the basics to get started. Items like seeds, plants, tools, water, manpower, chemicals, and cultivated rows. Plans on how, what, and where to plant are also necessary. The farmer also need to decide how to harvest the crop and what to do with the harvested crop. The next thing the farmer needs to do is understand the following:

- How to use each tool.

- How to properly use chemicals.

- How to plant the seeds.

- How the seeds will grow?

- How they will look.

- How to make rows.

- How to harvest the crop.

- How much of a harvest can be expected.

- How much time it will take from planting to harvest.

- The kind of soil.

- What the soil needs to make it fertile.

Likewise, specific environmental conditions are necessary to build and maintain high self-esteem.

These conditions may exist in varying degrees from household to household, but they are vital if a child is to develop into a healthy well-adjusted adult.

Only you can determine for your child to what degree these conditions can exist. There are no specific guidelines or recommendations on how much you should make these a part of your environment. However, the total absence of these environmental conditions will significantly reduce the chance of your child developing high self-esteem.

The five environmental conditions that will enhance the possibility of your child developing high self-esteem are:

Love bonds with significant others. Children must know they are loved for who they are—no strings attached. They have a bond between themselves and other members of the family or household.

A sense of belonging. Children want to feel that they have a place in their family. If children know that they are valued by significant others in their environment, they are less likely to seek out others that will allow them to be part of their group.

A sense of belonging is so important that you need to make every effort possible to create an environment where your children know they belong in a special way.

Acknowledged uniqueness. We enter this world with special and unique talents and gifts. These, in part, make us who we are. Acknowledging these gifts and talents will enhance self-esteem and help children appreciate who they are.

These talents and gifts can be used in many different ways, but if you want your children to have a full and productive life, they should be taught and encouraged to use their talents as tools of service.

Contributions. Allowing children to voice opinions and make suggestions will enhance self-esteem. They will know that you believe in their abilities to contribute if you provide these opportunities.

When suggestions are made by your child, every effort should be made to use some of them. Repeated rejection will lead to discouragement.

Appropriate models. Children are great imitators. What they see, they do. If you want your children to become responsible and mature citizens, you must model behaviors and attitudes that are socially acceptable and responsible.

It is not always easy to be an appropriate model for your children, but we must if we want the best for them and want them to be the best that they can be.

Being an appropriate model for your children is the best defense against remarks like, "How can you tell me not to, when you do it all the time?" "I saw you doing it."

I know what some of you are thinking right now, "My child does not have the right to talk to me that way." You are correct! But that will not stop them if you are setting a poor example. The children may not be making these remarks to be disrespectful. When there is a contradiction between what they are told and what they witness, they will become confused and question the discrepancy

What Now?

After a decision has been made about the degree to which you want specific environmental conditions to exist, a thorough understanding of each as they relate to your particular child and situation is vital. A lack of understanding may lessen a desire to bring about these conditions and may limit the extent in which you are able to effectively do so.

Once the gardener, decides what is needed, how much is needed, and understands what he must do to reap a bountiful harvest, he then moves on to assessment. He has to determine what is present and how this can be used to assist him in his efforts to bring about the best possible environment for growth. In addition, calculating what and how much he needs to add is critical.

You need to attempt to do the same. Unless you know how your children feel in relation to their environment and significant others, it is difficult to determine where to start.

Reviewing the section on "Indicators of High and Low Self-esteem" can help you in this task.

How Can These Conditions Be Brought About?

In order for these conditions to be brought about, certain elements need to be present. These elements will enhance the possibility that high self-esteem will take root, survive and thrive— even in adverse circumstances. The following list contains twenty-four of these elements. You should seek to add to this list as your knowledge increases.

- Have your children complete age appropriate chores daily/ weekly.

- Allow your children to accept responsibility for their actions.

- Spend time individually with each of your children.

- Teach your children how to solve problems.
    - ❏ Define the problem.
    - ❏ List all possible solutions.
    - ❏ List all parental and natural consequences for each solution.
    - ❏ Select the best solution.
    - ❏ Act.
- Have high expectations, but keep them realistic. Children live up or down to your expectations. If you expect them to do well, they probably will. If you expect them to perform poorly, they will do that as well.
- Believe in your child.
- Listen attentively to your child.
    - ❏ Stop what you are doing.
    - ❏ Look at your child.
    - ❏ Keep eye contact.
    - ❏ Acknowledge what your child is saying. You can do this by nodding your head or saying things like, "yes" and "I see what you are saying."
    - ❏ Sit in a "I'm really interested" posture.
- Allow your child to fail without saying that he or she is a failure for acting in that manner.
- Give your child a second chance. If the child fails the first time, let him or her try to perform the task again.
- Forgive your child for making mistakes.
- Accept your children as they are and work from there.
- Be aware of your own self-esteem. Children model what they see.
- Practice respect for your child.
- Provide clearly defined limits.

- Provide correction.

- Provide structure.

- Consistently enforce rules.

- Insist that your child finish what is started.

- Help your child set realistic goals.

- Encourage your child to try new things.

- Teach your child what is needed to be successful.

- Focus on your child's strengths.

- Love your child unconditionally.

- Provide positive feedback. We tend to give only negative feedback to children. We are very quick to tell them what they are doing wrong, but slow to praise them.

Things That Will Hinder the Development of High Self-Esteem or Destroy it in a Child

Lack of respect for each other. Children learn how to respect themselves and others from significant people in their lives. If these important and influential people do not respect each other, opportunities for children to learn this important life skill will be reduced. When children see this mutual respect, they are more apt to adopt the attitude that respect for oneself and others is vital to high self-esteem and healthy relationships.

Being inconsistent. When a parent is inconsistent with discipline, with love, with behavior, or with anything that has a direct bearing on a child, the child develops a sense of insecurity.

This feeling of insecurity often leads to low self-esteem. Consequently, inappropriate and inconsistent behaviors on the part of the child will follow.

Playing the role of the victim. Everette saw herself as a victim in almost every situation. She would ask, "Why me?" She would say, "I knew it was too good to be true. I am surprised my luck lasted this long." Finally, she would end up ignoring and avoiding everyone and everything.

Her behavior suggested to her children that everything which happened to her was someone else's fault and she had no control over her life. Someone was either responsible for making her happy or for making her sad. When she behaved in this manner, there were always lots of people around to console her. They would also assist her in the portrayal of the victim role by identifying and/or ridiculing the chosen villain.

By the time Everette's children reached the third grade, they too were blaming everything that happened to them on others. They rarely took responsibility for what happened in their lives.

Everette may have gotten a lot of mileage out of playing the victim, but her children paid dearly for it.

Problem transplant. Deal with the problem at hand. Once a problem is handled, forget it! Avoid reminding the child of it after it has been laid to rest.

Demanding perfection. Children are not perfect. If they were, they would not need you to instruct and guide them.

Demand excellence but not perfection! We had been experiencing some problems with loud talking in our school cafeteria. A teacher asked me to make suggestions on how to help eliminate this problem. I proposed that she allow her students to make pictures of persons depicting, "Sh-sh-sh-sh-sh-" to remind the students to keep the noise down.

She agreed for her class to make the pictures. Two days later, I was invited to view their work. I was very impressed with the pictures she had displayed on the table. The students did a great job. The pictures illustrated exactly what we had in mind.

After viewing the pictures on the table, she turned to some of the other students and said, "Those of you who had to do yours over, take them out of your desk and let her see them." I was floored! At this point I should have said something to save these students the embarrassment of showing their rejected pictures to me, but I didn't. I went along with this unnecessary assault on the children's self-esteem.

She took me to each of the students as they slowly and awkwardly pulled their pictures from their desks. All looked fine to me and I told them so.

I remember one of the students very vividly. She reluctantly slid her picture out of her desk. The teacher immediately said, "Hers was too wrinkled at the top." I thought, "What wrinkles?" The wrinkles were so few, she had to point them out to me. **Demand excellence, not perfection!**

Expecting the child to fail. "Daddy may I go outside and play some baseball?" asked Tyre. "No, you will not be able to hit that ball and you will only get hurt. You need more practice," replied Daddy.

This is just a typical example of how expecting failure can interfere with a child developing high self-esteem.

If we think the child will fail and express or act in ways that convey this, the child will be reluctant to try new things. If the child lacks the confidence to tackle new challenges, he or she will not experience many successes. When achievements are few, self-esteem tends to be low.

Now, of course we cannot allow children to try things that they are not mature enough (physically or mentally) to handle. But we can tell them in a way that does not have a negative impact upon them. Remember, it is not what you say all of the time, but how you say it.

Focusing exclusively on the negative. Children will make many mistakes as they struggle to become what they are created to be, but children will also do some pretty terrific things as well.

If you focus only on the times when your children mess up and ignore the ones when they behave in positive and responsible ways, you miss the opportunity to build on their strengths as well as provide a boost to their self-esteem.

Mistakes should be called to the attention of your children. However, when you do this, it should be done in a way that allows them to maintain their dignity while at the same time encourage them to examine the why, what, and how of the mistakes.

If you pay more attention to what your children do right, they will have incentive to choose positive behavior more frequently than the negative.

Two important things to remember: you cannot raise a *positive child* from *negative feedback,* and mistakes provide opportunities to teach for the parents and to learn for the children.

Although it maybe hard at times, you must make an effort to say at least one positive thing to your children each day. If you fail to do so, you will not be pleased with the final results.

Smothering a child. Children need room to grow physically, spiritually, socially, and emotionally. You may think you are giving and providing these opportunities to a degree necessary for growth. However, a closer look may reveal you are not.

I will never forget an incident that happened with my first child when I was pregnant with my second.

My church Sunday School Class had planned a baby shower for me. When it was time for the cake and food to be served, I put a cup with some drink in one hand and a small saucer with cake in the other of my child. To my astonishment he could not hold the two items. He wasted the drink and the cake fell from the plate.

I was so embarrassed. He was seven years old and he could not perform these simple tasks. As I looked around at the other children his age and even younger, I realized that he was the only one having problems with this. I knew I had to do something.

I had to ask myself why and how could I have allowed this to happen and not be aware of it. As I searched my memory and retraced past history, I realized he did not know because I never allowed him to grow in this area. I would always hold his drink or he would not take one if he had to hold it himself.

From that day forward, I started allowing him to do more for himself. Needless to say, I did not make the same mistake with my other two children.

Allowing and encouraging children to grow and expand as age and maturity dictates, will enhance self-esteem and promote responsibility.

Figuring out what to encourage at the various ages can be a monumental task if you do not have any direction or experience.

Many psychologists have devoted an enormous amount of time to studying which skills a child should be able to perform at various ages. I encourage you to find such a book on this topic. Keep in mind these should be viewed as possibilities not absolutes. There will always be exceptions to the rule.

There are human resources which I consider very valuable—successful veteran mothers and fathers. These people have the know how, experience and the benefit of hind sight. If you really want to do it right, seek these people out. They can be a tremendous help.

It is crucial that children be allowed to grow and experience new challenges. However, you should be aware that permitting them to expand and grow prematurely will put them at great risk of being involved in situations that are unsafe and/or unhealthy. In other words, you do not want to overprotect but you don't want to be too permissive. Determining where one ends and the other begins is the task.

Lack of respect for your child. Children are people too. They feel embarrassed, they get angry, they feel hurt, and so forth. Everything you feel, they feel too. Show respect for them. A lack of respect for children will cause them to become angry and discouraged. If you respect them, they will respect you, themselves, and others.

Part Four:
Encouragement

Encouragement breeds success.

What Does It Mean to Encourage?

There are times when you meet someone and flames of compassion seem to saturate every fiber of your being because of the experiences being shared with you. For me, May 5, 1993 was one of these times. A young lady, we will call her Melissa, peeked into my office and with a sad voice asked, "Are you busy?" "I need to talk with someone." Immediately I thought, "This is going to be one of those long ones. Maybe I'll have her come back at a more convenient time." "I will have finished with this paper work on my desk." I reasoned. But before I could get another word out, tears as free flowing as I had ever witnessed began dripping from her face. Needless to say, I put the paper work aside, grabbed the tissues, and invited her to be seated.

It took a few minutes for Melissa to regain her composure. Slowly and bashfully raising her head, she began to tell me a story that lasted over two hours.

Melissa started with her years spent in a house with a mother that was an alcoholic and an absent father. She painfully recalled the times in which her mother was insanely drunk, yelling obscenities and referring to her by names such as: stupid, worthless, good for nothing, whore, dummy, and ugly. Her mother never apologized for these things because she could not remember these bizarre and horrible episodes after sobering up. She said that as bad as this was, the worst thing she recalled is that she never heard the words, "I love you."

Melissa endured this kind of treatment from her mother for ten years. Then on one rainy day, the Department of Children Services showed up at her door. She tried desperately not to let the worker in. She feared what would happen if she saw the house in such a mess. Clothes everywhere, cigarettes butts all over the floor, and very little to eat in the refrigerator. But her insistence that nothing was wrong did not convince the worker to leave. The worker coaxed her into opening the door explaining that a neighbor had called about the living conditions. She has not lived with her mother since that day nor does she remember her mother trying to contact her.

Melissa spent the next five years with an elderly couple who appeared on the surface to be the model parents. They attended church, dressed her well, lavished her with a variety of expensive foods, and provided recreational activities. The general public thought they were wonderful to her and often told her how lucky she was. Lucky all right! Somehow she didn't feel very lucky when she recalled how many times this kind old man came into her room forcing her to do all sorts of things with him and to him.

Somehow the authorities found out and she now lives in a group home for girls. This is her fourth week in school, and she has not made any friends and teachers respond to her as though she has some sought of disease. This has been the story of her life—rejection and abuse. She feels worthless. Right now she feels like ending it all.

After such a disturbing and heart wrenching disclosure, what could I say? How should I respond? All the words in my vocabulary seemed inadequate. We sat in silence. After 15 minutes she said she felt strong enough to face the world again. She thanked me for my time and for listening. I invited her to return as often as she wanted or if she needed to check in with me the next day.

The next story is not as disturbing but helps to demonstrate the importance of encouragement.

Tai was uneasy about the upcoming baseball championship game. She was not sleeping, eating or concentrating on anything other than the game that was two weeks away.

Her team, the Falcons, had won fifteen games and lost five. The opposing team, the Tigers, had won sixteen games and lost 4. The Tigers had a pitcher that could throw a ball ninety miles an hour. Tai, the Falcon's pitcher, was good but could only throw eighty-five miles an hour. It was this five miles an hour difference that worried her.

A week before the game, Tai spent a lot of time reflecting on her progress since she started playing. She ended her first season pitching twenty-five miles per hour. From all indications, she had no talent as a pitcher and would never make a good one, but her coach believed in her abilities and helped her build confidence in them. No matter how terrible she was pitching, he would always tell her things like, "I know you are frustrated now, but you are going to be a great pitcher one day. Keep trying. You have the talent and the God given ability. It will take hard work, but you will get there." It was indeed this hard work and long hours of practice which helped her exceed her goal of being able to pitch seventy-five miles an hour by the end of her second season.

The big day finally arrived. Tai felt a little better about it now. She spent three hours a day practicing hard for the last two weeks. Her dedication and determination paid off. Now she is able to pitch a ball ninety-five miles an hour.

As she prepared to go on the field, her coach called her, put his hands on her shoulders, looked her square in the eyes, and said, "Win or lose, this is going to be the best game of the season. Have fun on the field."

It was these words which helped Tai pitch the last and best game of her four year high school career. When she heard those words, she experienced an overwhelming sense of relief. No matter what happened—win or lose—she would still have the support and respect of her friend—the coach.

Encouragement plays a tremendous role in the discovery and the development of gifts and talents. It is also a critical element in the development of a well adjusted child.

According to Webster, encouragement means to cheer, hearten, impel, support, inspire, and exhilarate. All of these words are significant and important. They tell us that to encourage someone means to empower ones own sense of belief. In other words, you help them to see, to find, to seek, and to use abilities and resources that were given to them at birth.

As individuals uncover these talents, they will begin to have a sense of control and the strength to do what they need to do to be successful. Young children are no different. They need to feel that they have sufficient power to control their behaviors and attitudes as well. They must also believe that they possess the strength to do so.

Does It Matter?

Think of a time when someone said something to you that completely burst your bubble. Perhaps you had worked on a project and you thought it was great. When you showed it to others you got comments like, "Interesting," "You must have worked hard on this." These comments were kind ones, but you knew by their action and tone of voice that they thought it as crummy. Children are no different.

Encouragement plays a tremendous role in how we perceive our talents and abilities now and what we will do with them in the future. Many people have failed to be, what they want to be, because someone discouraged them.

Does it matter? It matters a great deal. For the most part, children believe and behave the way they think that you think they ought to. That is why you must be careful in choosing what kind of message you send to your children through actions and words. These can be powerful tools of encouragement. On the other hand, if used in a negative way they can be just as discouraging.

A Starting Place

When it is time to do anything, this question ultimately comes up—Where do I start? No matter what the project may be or what is involved, the one common element is you; you start with yourself.

As a counselor, I have had many opportunities to work with a great number of students and their parents. I have seen encouraged children and discouraged ones. I think it is important for parents to examine how and why their words and actions encourage or discourage children.

A good place to start is to look at behaviors and words which encourage and discourage. You may want to evaluate how you rate on each.

In most cases, encouraged children live in environments which provide generous amounts of the following:

- Praise.
- Parental body language that says to the child, you are somebody.
- Positive overt acts (kindness, smile, hugs, and kisses).
- Helping attitude on the part of the parent.
- Parents who listen with interest.
- Commitment to the child.
- Faith in the child.
- Love for the child.
- Trust in the child.
- Parents as appropriate role models.
- Appropriate, sound, and consistent discipline.
- Forgiving attitude on the part of the parents.
- Sense of belonging.
- Positive parental expectations.

- Clear rules and limits.
- Opportunities to voice opinions in appropriate settings.
- Opportunities to do for themselves.
- Immediate and specific information about task performance.
- Acknowledgment and encouragement for unique qualities.
- Acknowledgment of effort.
- Daily and weekly chores performed on a regular basis.
- Acknowledgment for small accomplishments.

In most cases, children that are discouraged have experienced the following in excessive amounts:

- Negative feedback.
- Negative overt acts (cruelty, frowns, etc.).
- Passive listening on the part of the parent.
- Negative parental expectations.
- Hopelessness on the part of the parent.
- Unforgiving attitude on the part of the parent.
- Inconsistent discipline.
- Unclear rules and limits.
- Lack of faith in the child.
- Inappropriate role models.
- Lack of trust on the part of the parents.
- Feeling unloved by parents.
- Parents' unwillingness to provide help and guidance.
- Unacknowledged accomplishments.
- Parents do for the child what the child can do for him or herself.
- Lack of immediate and specific feedback about a performance.

- Failure of parents to acknowledge individuality.

- Lack of chores.

- Failure of parents to acknowledge effort.

- Lack of encouragement to try new and different things.

- Only large accomplishments acknowledged.

There is not a parent anywhere who does all of the first list and none of the second one. If there is, we need to find that parent so he/she can tell us how to be perfect. Neither is there a parent who does all of the second list and none of the first.

All parents have some strengths and weaknesses. As long as parents are willing to build upon the strengths and to modify or change attitudes and behaviors which cripple, damage, defeat, or discourage, they are on a good road to becoming the best that they can be.

Each parent is a different individual, no two people will do things the same way. The method in which you perform a task is not necessarily wrong or right—it is different. It is okay to be different as long as you do not hurt others or yourself. The aim should be to perform in a manner which would be most beneficial to the child.

Behaving in ways which yield the best results is what encouraging parents do well. Therefore, performing as many task as possible on the first list will help you to move closer to becoming the best parent that you can be. As a result, you will have a child with the courage to withstand peer pressure, make good decisions, build healthy relationships, be a successful student, and most of all, be a productive and responsible member of society.

You should work diligently to provide needed encouragement to each of your children. Often you have to behave in a certain way with one child while at the same time you may have to reach into your bag of assorted parenting skills to find the most appropriate method to respond to another. Remember, one way does not work with all children.

What Does It All Mean?

In order for you to fully understand each of these encouraging and discouraging behaviors and which one you use the most, an examination of each is necessary.

Related amounts of positive feedback. "Good going." "Great." "Terrific." "Wonderful." These are some of the things children should hear from you so that they will know how they are doing. However, you should be aware that too much of anything is counterproductive.

Children can become praise addicts if praise is given for every little thing. Pretty soon, children will perform only when they believe praise will be forthcoming. Children should be praised in a unpredictable manner, yet genuine and motivating.

If a child ties his or her shoe laces for the first time, praise can be motivating when given in a genuine way. If however, this is the tenth time the child has tied his or her shoe laces and you still find yourself responding with, "You tied your shoe laces, great!" and the child every time says, "Look Mommie, I tied my shoe laces," praise has become predictable.

Then there is the flip side of the coin—no praise at all or limited amounts of praise. It is crucial that children hear words which will motivate them. When this does not happen, children have no way of knowing if their behavior is acceptable. Praise is the kind of feedback which can help children discover their strengths and build high self-esteem.

Body language. Body language accounts for 50 percent of communication. In view of this, tone of voice, words you say, and the manner in which you say them need to communicate the same message. If you say, "I love you" but the expression on your face does not say the same thing, the child will doubt your sincerity.

Your body language determines if your child believes what you say.

Immediate and specific feedback. Immediate and specific feedback for the performance of a task can be thrilling to the ears of a child. "You started dinner without me asking, thanks." "You completed your homework in plenty time to play, great." "You ate your corn without making a fuss, terrific!" "You played with your sister 20 minutes and you didn't fight, wonderful!" "You cleaned your room without pouting, good going!"

Praise coupled with specific details about why the behavior is acceptable will tell children what they can do the next time to be successful. "Great job" and "Good work" do not indicate what was done to make it good or great. Give children as much information as possible when praising them.

Positive overt action. The way you behave with your children has a profound effect on them. If you smile, treat them with kindness, hug them, kiss them, or hold their hands, they will accept themselves as being worthwhile human beings. This will encourage them to treat others in the same way. They will also feel accepted by you and they will know that you love them no matter what.

Positive overt actions should take place when things are going great as well as when things are not going so well. It is important to do this so that your children will know "good or bad," they are loved.

Helping attitude. "I don't know how to do this." "I have to make an 86 on this test to bring my grade up to a C." "I want to make a cake but I don't know how." "This boy is bothering me at school and I don't know how to handle it."

We can go on and on with these kind of statements. Children often have problems that they need help with. Knowing that you are there to help them when they need it, provides a sense of security.

A helping attitude toward your children encourages them to tackle new and difficult tasks and to meet challenges with confidence.

Parents who listen. In order to listen, you have to decide to do so. It is a conscious effort. We *hear* all the time, but we do not always *listen*. I have had the experience of riding in my car with the radio playing and not knowing what was being said or what music was playing. It is the same way with your children; you have to decide to focus your attention on them.

Children know when they are being listened to, just like you know. When children feel that you care enough about them to listen, they will begin to share more and more with you.

If your children begin to talk and it is not a good time, ask them to wait until you are able to listen. If you are in the middle of finishing up something that needs to be completed right away, you can say something like: "I really must finish this or it will be ruined." "I want to be able to really listen to what you have to say." "Give me a few minutes, then we can talk."

Commitment. It is said that a committed person is a faithful person. Your children need to feel that you are committed to helping them become the best they can be in whatever they are involved in.

We know that the older a child becomes, the more active they will be. They will become involved in sports, organizations, and so forth. Whatever the case may be, they should have the assurance that you will be there to assist them with your presence, time, money, and moral support.

This is not an easy thing to do, but who said it was easy? Many sacrifices will have to be made. However, by doing so, your children will learn that sacrifices made for others are worthy and fulfilling. Beyond this, they certainly will appreciate the sacrifices you make for them. Many people get nervous when they hear the word—sacrifice. I do not know how you can be committed without being willing to sacrifice.

Faith and trust. These two words go hand and hand. Without faith in someone you will not trust them. It is crucial that your children feel that you have faith in them. When they believe that you trust them, they will behave in responsible ways.

Many parents operate under the mistaken notion that distrust will keep children in line. They believe that if their children are aware of this lack of faith, they will not do anything that would cause disapproval. On the contrary, children will rebel against this kind of attitude by doing the very thing you do not want them to do.

Trust your children unless they give you reasons not to. Even then, allow them an opportunity to earn that trust back. You may want to start very small and build to bigger things.

As your children work to gain your trust, encourage them along the way. Children want to be trusted by their parents. They act like they do not care or it does not matter, but they need and want your trust. Besides, they know if you do not trust them, the less they will get to do.

W.I.S.E. parents (Wisdom, Involved, Sincere, Empowering) role models. Children are great imitators. What they see, they do. It is up to you to model behaviors and attitudes that will help your children become responsible and mature adults.

Some examples of what you need to model if you want to be WISE and effective are:

- Healthy lifestyles.

- Expected and accepted behavior.

- Positive values.

- Wholesome attitudes.

- High self-esteem.

- Responsibility.

- How to be a good teacher so they will be able to teach their children. A good teacher:

  ❏ Breaks down tasks into small steps so a child can perform each step.

  ❏ Makes clear how performance will be evaluated.

  ❏ Provides evaluations that include feedback about what was done correctly and incorrectly.

  ❏ Works with the child to solve any problems.

- Sincerity and honesty.

- Love.

- Patience.

- Commitment.

- Faith.

- Trust.

Discipline

This word usually brings the word "spanking" to mind. Discipline is more than this. It is helping your children to develop and grow in all areas—socially, emotionally, physically, and spiritually. Sometimes spankings are necessary, but by no means should spankings be used exclusively, abusively, or vindictively. To learn more about this topic, refer to the section on discipline.

Love

What can be said about love? It is the most powerful encourager in the entire universe. You can do all you want to do to help your child, but if your child does not feel loved, it is all futile.

It is important that you demonstrate your love for your children because they learn to love themselves and others from you. Love requires some action. Feeling love for someone means little if you never show it.

It is critical that you love yourself so that you are able to love your child. You can only give what you have. If you have loneliness, you will give loneliness. If you have happiness, you will give happiness. If you have anxiety, you will give anxiety. Examine yourself to see where you are. If you are not where you need to be in order to model love, then do something about it.

Whatever you do, don't cheat yourself or your child out of having this experience. Without it, life means very little and is very discouraging.

     Educational Media Corporation®

Love includes but is not limited to the following:

- Understanding
- Patience
- Peace
- Light
- Commitment
- Unselfishness
- Self-control
- Access to you

- Hope
- Joy
- Faith
- Discipline
- Grace
- Empathy
- Forgiveness
- Self-discovery

A Feeling of Hopelessness

Hope makes the soul assured,

that whatever happens,

everything is most secured

Hope pulls back the curtain—that darkens the mind,

and shine a light on things—you would not otherwise find

Without hope you will see,

the things you most want will cease to be,

dreaming, striving, planning, and growing,

make everything keep flowing

Don't lose hope—it is a waste,

to give up—even a taste

Your attitude will influence, to a great extent, how your children participate in this drama called life.

You need to be keenly aware that children are watching your every move, and they are not watching for nothing. They plan to use the information gathered over the years to structure their lives. Your life serves as a guide to them. While they may not adopt all of your values and beliefs, they will integrate a great deal of them into their own lives. Now, if you could choose which they adopt, that would be wonderful. You probably would select the ones you have used successfully over the years. However, children have their own minds and their own wills. They will pick the values they want. It is for this reason that you have to be very careful about the kind of lifestyle you live in the presence of your children.

Striving to make things better (economically, emotionally, socially relationally, etc.) planning for the future, seeking skill and knowledge, having a desire to accomplish other things, finding good where there seems to be none, having an upbeat outlook on life, and settling only for the very best, are attitudes and attributes that will help children see life as a challenge that can be met with varying degrees of success.

On the other hand, if you have a pessimistic view of life, finding fault with everything, willing to settle for less than the best of life, and having no plans for the future, you will demonstrate to your children that life is hopeless and there is nothing they can do to make things better. If children adopt this attitude, you will have another generation that will live out their lives in despair. This life of hopelessness will lead to an unfulfilled, discouraged, unsuccessful, and unproductive existence.

Remember, children are great imitators. If you live your life in a hopeless manner , do not be surprised if your children do the same. It is wise for you to keep in mind that children with hope are children with courage. As The Reverend Jessie Jackson puts it, "Keep hope alive." By doing so, you will give your children a gift that can be passed down to many generations. You are going to leave your children an inheritance. Which would you rather leave them, hope or hopelessness? You decide!

Is Being Connected Important?

You bet! Children need to know that they have a place in your heart and your life. A feeling of being connected to someone or/ and something gives them a sense of identity. If children feel disconnected from their significant others, they will seek out others which allow them to be part of their world. When this happens, who they become will largely be influenced by who or what they perceive themselves being linked to.

It is crucial that children (especially teens because of their vulnerability to peer pressure and their struggle to establish their own identity) know that they occupy a special position with you and within the family.

I hope once again we will see people living in a community, city, town, or street with that sense of connectedness that was evident not so long ago. I remember how the entire community took responsibility for all children where I grew up—Trio, SC. They were able to discipline if the situation warranted it and they would most certainly tell the parents. As a child, it was hard to see where this kind of "Community Parenting" was benefiting me. However, when I became a parent, I wished that more of the same existed so my children could be recipients. This kind of "we-ness" gave children a unique opportunity to experience what it meant to belong on a broader scale. Today, if a adult attempts to discipline a child in the community, that person has to deal with the possibility of a law suit.

There may be very little you can do about "Community Parenting," but there is a lot that you can do about making your children feel that they belong to you and your family. They should know that nothing will separate them from your love—Nothing! When children feel that they are connected, they will be able to deal courageously with the most difficult circumstances in life. Self-esteem is certain to improve if this feeling of connectedness is continuously reinforced.

Positive Expectations

Cindy wanted to play the piano. She talked with her mother about the possibility. Her mother thought about it for awhile and said, "Learning to play the piano takes hard work and a lot of time. I don't know if you are up to the challenge."

Across America many parents are responding to their children's ideas and requests in the same manner. Parents, for the most part, do not mean to say things that will have a devastating effect on children, but these kinds of remarks are made every day. If Cindy's mother was concerned about her child not being able to stick to the task of learning to play the piano, a better response would have been something like, "You seem to be interested in learning how to play. Let me ask a few questions. How many times a week will you need to practice? Will this interfere with any of the activities with which you are currently involved? Will this limit the time you have for study? How much practice time will you need at home?"

Along with asking questions, Cindy's mother may have wanted to give her opinion in a non-judgmental way. By doing it this way, Cindy would know that she retains the privilege to have input into the decision. In most cases, when done in the proper way, children will do the right thing.

"Take this and put it in the trash can. Please be careful—you know how careless you can be sometimes." Statements like these are examples of having negative expectations of your child. You expect the child to perform poorly and the child lives down to your expectations. How would you feel if someone said this to you? Children feel the same way when things like these are said to them—discouraged. Children are as much human as grown-ups are. They have the same feelings and emotions. We, as a society, and you, as parents, must remember this if we want children to grow into responsible and encouraged individuals.

Expecting bad things from your children and communicating this to them weakens the self-esteem of a child and causes them to believe they "can't do anything right."

Show your children that you believe they can get the job done, whatever that job may be. Children will not always be 100% successful. However, success on any level needs to be recognized and commended, especially if it is a new task. If it is not a new one, they still may not be 100% triumphant. When this happens, you can show support by encouraging them to stick with it. This will let your children know that you still have faith in them and their ability to perform.

Negative expectations destroy a child's self-confidence and prevents a wholesome relationship from forming between parent and child.

Rules and Limits

Clear rules and limits give children a sense of connectedness and eliminate confusion and chaos.

Children need and should have clear and specific rules and limits. These are necessary so that children will not be confused about what behaviors are or are not expected or acceptable.

Unclear rules and limits only make for chaos. Children will often challenge you if the rules and limits are not spelled out and have not been made plain to them. For example, you told your children that they could play in the yard. You look out of the window to find them in the front yard. You go outside and scold them by saying, "I told you to play only in the back yard." The children look at you confused and respond, "No Mommie, You told us that we could play in the yard." Do not expect your children to read your mind and fill in the missing blanks. Be very clear on what you want or expect from them.

Whatever your rules and limits are, be certain that your children understand them. It is also important that you don't have rules and limits that you have problems sticking to. For example: Danny wanted to watch the most important football game of the season in the den. You have told him that under no circumstances is he to eat in the den. After several minutes of pleading, you give in. However, you caution him that this will not happen again. That caution means nothing. Danny will ask again. Do not make rules that you have not thought through. Say what you mean and mean what you say.

Once the children know what your rules and limits are and that you are committed to making sure they adhere to them, they will respect and abide by them.

Clear rules and limits give children a sense of connectedness and eliminate confusion, and chaos. This will boost children's self-esteem and produce adults that are responsible human beings. After all, in the end—isn't that what we want?

Contributions

It is important that children feel they have something to contribute. By asking their opinions and listening to suggestions that they offer, will let them know that you value what they think.

Children must also understand you reserve the right to make the final decision. Nonetheless, every effort should be made to implement some of their suggestions. If your children's suggestions or opinions are never taken, they will become discouraged and feel that they do not have anything worth accepting.

I am not speaking about major matters in the household. Things such as: what to have for dinner, what story they want to hear, what to wear to school, how to get all the groceries in the house in one trip, what movie to see, and so forth, are appropriate.

Teenagers, however, may be able to understand matters that are much more significant than deciding on a movie. They are often very helpful in offering suggestions and possible solutions in situations such as where to move furniture or where to shop. You have to determine what your children are ready for and what they can handle.

Don't Do for a Child What the Child Can Do for Himself or Herself

> *Allowing and insisting your children do for themselves what they can do will strengthen their belief in their ability to perform and will encourage them to face new challenges with a sense of expectancy and accomplishment.*

"I'll help you." "Come here and let me do it for you." "Bring it here, I'll do it for you." Statements and actions like these tell children that they do not need to worry about doing anything that will cause them any degree of discomfort because everything will be taken care of for them.

When you do this, children soon learn that all they have to do is complain about the task being too difficult. When you rescue your children from facing challenges and solving problems, you undermine their potential to grow, become effective problem solvers and to be responsible citizens.

Allowing and insisting your children do for themselves what they can do, will strengthen their belief in their ability to perform and will encourage them to face new challenges with a sense of expectancy and accomplishment.

You must also remember that it is easier to do things for children even after they have learned a skill. I often wanted to wash my four year old's face, a skill that she had mastered nicely. She quickly reminded me that she could do it herself. She was not so swift to remind me that she could cut her hot dog with a fork. Why was this the case? This task was much more difficult for her, and she would have preferred me to handle it.

Do yourself and your children a favor, do not do for them what they can do for themselves. I hear some parents complaining about still having to do for their children even after they are grown. A little investigation usually reveals that the children were never made to do things that were clearly appropriate and feasible. Children, like grown ups, are creatures of habit. Once a behavior becomes part of a person, it is difficult to alter or change that behavior. It is not impossible, but it is difficult.

Unique Qualities are Acknowledged and Encouraged

* *
Each of us was born unique,
It's these things that we should seek,
Take the time to find and use,
The talents and gifts that can be news.
* *

We do not all come into this world with the same gifts and talents.. Each of us were born a unique individual. We were born with talents and gifts that only we can use in this world. If we fail to use them or even find out what they are, the world will miss a great contribution that only we can give.

Many people are born and die without ever knowing their purpose for being; without ever discovering their uniqueness. This is very tragic and is such a great waste. Think about it—if someone is born for the express purpose of discovering a cure for a dreaded disease and that person failed to utilize this gift, thousands or millions of people could die because of this. If a person is born to bring sunshine into the lives of many by wearing a smile and using laughter, what happens if he or she does not? If a person is born to be a great cook and decides not to make that a part of his or her life, someone would miss the pleasure of eating some fabulous food

Since each person is born with unique talents and gifts, it is your responsibility to acknowledge and encourage your children to utilize their God given gifts. One child may a have musical talent; another may have signs of being a scientist; another may have a way with children; another may have the ability to grow things. Whatever the talent, you should recognize and support your children's use of it.

You may find it difficult not to compare one child with another. But, remember this is very counterproductive and will only make children angry and discouraged. Instead of doing this, seek to find areas of strength in each child and cultivate them.

I am not proposing that weaknesses in children should not be addressed. Clearly, if some areas of weakness are not strengthened, children will have a difficult time participating in other functions successfully. For example, if a child is disorganized, (things always out of place, loses things, etc.) his or her classroom experience will be frustrating at best. It is important that you work with your children on matters that would cause them discouragement, frustration, and poor self-esteem.

Talents and Gifts

Take a moment to complete the activity below. You may discover some interesting things about your children. Read it daily.

Child's Name

_____

Talents/gifts

1. _____

2. _____

3. _____

Ways to acknowledge these talents/gifts

1. _____

2. _____

3. _____

Ways to encourage these talents/gifts

1. _____

2. _____

3. _____

Efforts and Small Accomplishments are Acknowledged

A basketball player scores 100 points in a game. A student makes all A's on a report card. A child sets the table perfectly for dinner. A student makes 100 on a spelling test. Society typically recognizes great achievement at the expense of small accomplishments and efforts. Few people will take note of a child working hard to make a 100 on a spelling test but falls short by 30 points. This same child made only 50s and 60s one year ago. For this child, this was quite an achievement. A child learning how to ride a bike would benefit from some acknowledgment of each small step mastered. If the child learns how to sit on the bike correctly the first time, that is worthy of notice and encouragement.

It is each successive step that eventually yields the end product. If there is no encouragement or acknowledgment for each step, the end product may never come about or will be delayed. A person builds a house one brick at a time. If the person decides not to lay the last 15 bricks required to complete the house, that house will never be finished. A dress is made one seam at a time. If a person decides to sew only the first seam, the dress will not be in wearable condition until all the necessary seams are made. A car is built one bolt or piece at a time. If the manufacture neglects to put all necessary bolts in the motor of a car, the car will have problems functioning at its optimum. A tree grows one inch at a time. If a tree does not receive proper amounts of water and sun, it will soon be stunted or die. If this happens, that tree will never grow to it's full height.

So it is with children, they grow one step at a time. It is imperative that they are given the right amounts of acknowledgment and encouragement for little things. If parents do this, their children's self-esteems will be enhanced. This positive way in which they feel about and see themselves will, in time, motivate them to reach their full potential.

Ask any successful person and they will tell you that someone encouraged and believed in them every step of the way. You can be that person to your children.

Child Performs Chores on a Regular Basis

I was raised on a farm. My parents planted everything from corn to cucumbers. We never had to wonder about what we would do for the Summer. We already knew—work! My parents never had the pleasure of hearing the words "I'm bored." We were very aware that if we dared to utter those words they would have been delighted to swiftly and creatively fill our lives with exciting work.

Society has changed dramatically over the past decade: both parents work outside the home, children are in daycare or afterschool care more than they are in the presence of their parents, and children are asked to assume less responsibility around the house. The list could go on and on. It is because of these changes that parents need to be aware of the importance of teaching children good and sound work ethics.

These valuable ethics will help children perform in a conscientious and productive manner. When children are achieving, they experience a tremendous boost to their self-esteem. It is this favorable opinion of themselves that will enable them to overcome obstacles and to reach short and long term goals.

One way of teaching children the importance of good work ethics and how fruitful and fulfilling it makes one feel is to assign daily chores. The following should be considered before chores are designated:

- The age of the child.

- How much time is involved in completing the chore? How long (30 minutes, one year, two weeks, four months, etc.) will the child be expected to perform the task?

- When will the child be required to perform the task?

- Can the child complete the task without help?

- Will the task require supervision?

- Who will supervise the task if supervision is required?

- How often will the child be required to perform the task?

If your children are not accustomed to doing chores, start with small weekly tasks and add more as they adapt to this new phenomenon in your household.

A chore chart, in the beginning, would be helpful as a way of reminding them when the tasks need to be completed. This chart can be as simple as writing the chores on a sheet of paper. If your child has not started reading, pictures may be drawn to represent the chore. However, as soon as possible, this chart should be phased out so that children will be encouraged to remember to do the chores on their own. Verbal reminders may also be necessary for awhile. This too should be eliminated as quickly as possible.

The chart should be displayed in a public place in the house, such as your refrigerator, and in the children's bedroom. It would not hurt to keep a copy on file someplace just in case both lists disappear.

After your children have mastered one task, assigning new or more challenging ones may be appropriate. The decision to do so should be based on the readiness of the children. Additional privileges should accompany more complex task. This will illustrate to the children that the acquisition of privileges is directly related to responsible completion of assigned chores. This further demonstrates that you believe in their ability to handle more challenging assignments. This lesson will serve them well in the work force. They will remember that if a task is completed in a timely, ethical, and productive manner, more responsibility along with increased privileges will be given.

Forgiving Attitude

Mistakes that are made by children offer parents wonderful opportunities to teach.

Children make mistakes. This is a fact that will be with us as long as children are with us. When children do make mistakes, we are prone to yell, scold, and accuse them of being insensitive, unthinking and careless. When we react in this manner, we produce discouraged children with poor self-esteem that lack the confidence to try new things and to make sound decisions.

Now, your question may be, "How do I know when my children are making an honest mistake or deliberately messing up?" You are smart. For the most part, you can tell which child did what, what time it was done, how it was done, and why it was done. If I get up in the morning and discover a plate on the coffee table, I know that my oldest son ate something late that night and did not put the plate in the sink. If I go in to the boy's bathroom and lots of soft soap is in the sink, I know that my youngest son used too much, and that he tried to clean it up but was not successful. If I go into the pantry to get a box of noodles and there are none, I know to ask my daughter where they are. You know your children well enough to know when an honest mistake has occurred.

Mistakes that are made by children offer parents wonderful opportunities to teach. If parents view these as teachable moments rather than "You should have known better times," they can become learning experiences for the children. Think about it, if children were perfect, they would not need you. If they did not need you, you would not have a job. But, they are not perfect, and you do have a job. You are charged with the responsibility of assisting your children to grow to their fullest potential.

You are probably asking—how do I create these learning experiences? One way you can do this is by telling the child why you feel he or she has made a mistake. If the child accepts what you say, you stand a good chance of the mistake not being repeated. However, if the child rejects what you say, you probably will be addressing this same situation again. Another way is by asking open-ended questions about the mishap. When you do this, you are actually letting the child take responsibility for answering and thereby take responsibility for the behavior and the results of that behavior.

Some questions that you may include are:

- What happened?

- What was your part in it?

- What could you have done differently that would have made things better?

- Is there anything that you can do about it now?

Remember, these are only a few questions that you may want to ask. Questions will need to be tailored to the specific situation. "What," "how," and "is" words are very useful when using this technique.

In addition to asking questions when your children make mistakes, discussing consequences with your children at this time is appropriate and advised. It is beneficial for you and the children if they know what will happen if this behavior continues. It helps you because you will know exactly what you are going to do if it occurs again. It benefits the child because there will be no surprises. As you consider what consequence to utilize, refer to the guidelines in the section on discipline.

It is important to keep in mind that consequences should not be threats. That is why it is important that you say what you mean and do what you say. If you fail to do this, your children will view stated consequences as threats that they know you will not act upon. When this happens, your effectiveness is limited. Often when parents feel that they are no longer effective with their children, they become unforgiving. Every time their children make a mistake, the parents remind them of the one they made a year, month, week, or day ago.

This kind of attitude discourages children from taking responsibility for their action and frustrates parents to the point of saying, "If I can't maintain control, I can remind them of how they are always doing things wrong". This ultimately will lead to children who see themselves as unacceptable no matter what they do. The end product of this kind of relationship is children with poor self-esteem, irresponsible behavior, and poor decisions making skills. Children who continue in this way will often become adults that are unproductive citizens.

Have the same kind of attitude with your children as you want them to have with you—A FORGIVING ONE!

Do not expect miracles the first time you use these techniques. A child who has been resistant to taking responsibility for his or her behavior in the past, may need more work than a child who has not adopted this as part of his or her way of dealing with mistakes. But do not give up. Remember, this is a learned response and if it is learned, it can be unlearned. If you are consistent in using these techniques, they will yield a bountiful harvest. These are non-judgmental ways of allowing your child to admit mistakes in a safe and reassuring environment. Isn't that what we want children to do—accept responsibility for their behaviors?

Part Five: Responsibility?

The more responsible we are, the more we are satisfied with who we are.

What is Responsibility?

"Ramon never has paper, pencil, and rarely has books for class. Homework is turned in sporadically and often incomplete. However, he usually manages to pass his test with higher marks than his classmates. He is very capable but refuses to do the day to day activities needed to be successful."

This information was no surprise to Ramon's parents. They had observed the careless attention to their son's room and other household chores. Clothes were thrown everywhere, dishes half done, personal items lying around, and things not replaced after being used.

When asked how they addressed these behaviors at home, their responses were: the door to his bedroom was closed, mom picks up after him, both parents fussed a lot but with little or no results, and privileges were taken away until the pleading and asking for mercy wore them down.

This familiar story may lead one to ask, what is responsibility? How is responsibility taught? What can be done to get children to be responsible? Why do children avoid responsibility? How is responsibility avoided? How do we know when children are be-having in responsible ways?

These questions are not easy ones to answer. They challenge the most experienced parent. Each child is unique with an indi-vidual personality and set of norms. Therefore, parents, experi-enced and inexperienced, must continually seek ways to teach the life skill of responsibility to their children.

As parents search for strategies and techniques for teaching responsibility, they often find an array of programs or models that offer many helpful suggestions. As helpful as these are, the ques-tion of "How do I integrate this into everyday life?" still causes increased concern.

Taking responsibility should be an integral part of everyday life. Teaching responsibility in isolation can cause parents to be-come frustrated when the child fails to transfer the knowledge into practical living situations. It can also confuse the child about what is responsible behavior and what is not.

There are many views as to what being responsible is. Webster defines it as "Liable to answer for something; of good credit or position." The author of Active Parenting defines responsibility as "Choice + consequences." There are others who view responsibility as making decisions that will improve the quality of life for oneself and others.

These definitions are valid and have merit. Consequently, when all of them are combined and other components are added, a clearer picture of what responsibility is emerges.

Being responsible starts with the attitude of the person. The individual's attitude will effect how and what decisions are made. The outcome, what happens as a result of that decision, could be accepted or rejected by the person. If the individual owns up to making that decision, the consequences, good or bad, are readily received. However, the consequences may be rejected if the person decides to deny, blame, excuse, or justify the decision. If we bring all of these components together, the following formula emerges: **Attitude + Decisions + Ownership + Consequences = Responsibility.**

To Whom are We Responsible?

There is nothing that you can do that will affect only you. Any thing you do will directly or indirectly have a bearing on the life of someone else. For example, if you eat too much, you feel miserable but others have to listen to you complain. If you had plans with some people, you are not going to feel like carrying them out. Therefore, they will be disappointed.

At certain times in our lives we may be responsible to a number of different people. These may include our parents, supervisors, aunts, babysitters, teachers, preachers, and so forth.

While some of the people we are responsible to may change from time to time and from situation to situation, being responsible to God, others, and ourselves will never change.

Children need to learn very early that when they make decisions —good or bad—they will effect a host of other people. Therefore, they should try to make decisions that will enhance the quality of life for themselves as well as others.

Who is Responsible for Our Lives?

We are completely and totally responsible for our lives. The more responsible we are, the more we are satisfied with who we are. When we take responsibility, we greatly improve our chances of becoming the person we were created to be. As a result, our self-esteem will be enhanced.

When we fail to own up to our choices and refuse to accept the consequences of them, the likelihood of us developing to our fullest potential is reduced.

The lives of children will be tremendously changed if they are taught this at an early age and embraced truthfully by you.

Responsibility Fears!

There are several reasons why we do not accept responsibility for our actions. As many as these are, they commonly involve some element of fear.

We want others to think well of us; children are no different. If they do something that might jeopardize a favorable opinion of them, they become afraid of what others may think or do.

Through my work with children, I have been able to identify six of these fears that hinder or make it unattractive to accept responsibility for attitude, decisions, and behaviors.

FEAR #1—Afraid of Discipline

FEAR #2—Afraid of Being Blamed

FEAR #3—Afraid of A Friend or Peer Being Angry

FEAR #4—Afraid of Put Downs and Criticism

FEAR #5—Afraid of An Adult Being Angry

FEAR #6—Afraid of Not Being Accepted or Liked

These fears are often a result of previous interaction with significant others in their environment. Family members, friends, neighbors, teachers and others, frequently, though not intentionally, send out messages that say: "If you are not perfect, something is wrong with you."

Because the children often have more of the negative rather than the positive messages, children learn to be overly critical of themselves.

As a parent, you can help children to eliminate or deal with these fears by providing an environment of unconditional love. (Refer to the section on cooperation) Such a warm and accepting atmosphere will encourage children to be more responsible. They will know that although you do not approve of their behavior, you support and love them no matter what.

How Do We Avoid Responsibility?

Responsibility is avoided by doing the following four things:

1. Blaming others or circumstances. "You made me spill my drink." "If that pole was in a different place, I would have seen it."

2. Justifying. "What do you expect, I am a strong willed person." "Being late isn't such a big deal. Besides, I'm never late for really important stuff."

3. Making excuses. "I'm late because I got confused on the directions." "My alarm clock didn't go off."

4. Denying. "It wasn't me. It must have been someone else."

Trouble with Avoiding Responsibility!

When children avoid responsibility, they miss opportunities to learn from their mistakes. Thus, they tend to make the same ones over and over. If they repeatedly do this, becoming a responsible person is more difficult.

Children who are effective and satisfied are those who accept the consequences of their choices. Whether the consequences are positive or negative, they see them as opportunities for learning and growth.

Fifteen Principles for Teaching Responsibility

When you teach responsibility as an integral part of everyday life and allow these principles to guide your approach, teaching responsibility will be viewed as an exciting challenge rather than a dreaded part of parenting.

Listed below are fifteen principles that can be used as guidelines as you decide how you want to teach your children responsibility.

Model responsibility for your child. Children learn a great deal about acting in responsible ways from significant others around them. For example, if you spill something and turn to someone and say, "If you were not in the way, that would not have happened." Do not be too upset if your child does the same thing.

Some examples of other behavior children model are:

- Getting others to make decisions for them.
- Indecisiveness.
- Forgetting.
- Being late.
- Being manipulative.
- Selfishness.
- Greed.
- Kindness.
- Gentleness.
- Love.
- Patience.
- Faith.
- Jealousy.
- Deceit.
- Hate.
- Caring.

There are no strategies or techniques that will teach children how to be responsible if all they see from significant others is irresponsibility.

Children are great imitators. What they see, they do. It is up to you to model behaviors and attitudes that will help your children become responsible and mature adults.

Hold them accountable for their decisions. Children come up with all kinds of reasons and justification for not behaving in a responsible manner. Listen to their explanation, but do not buy in to it hook, line and sinker! They may say things like, "The only reason I hit my sister was because she was bothering me." "I didn't have time to make my bed because I had to watch this special show on TV for a class."

Allow children to experience consequences. If a child decides not to do homework, let the child be responsible for telling the teacher. Avoid running interference by writing a note so that the teacher will excuse the behavior.

Help children analyze what happened. Ask helpful questions. These questions should be designed to help the child examine the reasons for what happened. For example, What happened? What role did you play in this? Were there other ways it could have been handled? What could you have done differently? How did your behavior help the situation? How did your behavior hurt the situation?

Teach children patience. Many irresponsible responses and decisions are due to a lack of patience. Children do not have the patience to wait for answers, gratification or attention. They want it now!

Thoughtful people are patient people. Lack of patience breeds impulsiveness. Children behave in unrestrained ways because they do not take time to think about the consequences that may result.

How do we teach patience? There are several things that you can do to help develop patience in your child. A few of them are listed below:

- Model patience for your children. You are your children's mirror. Your children will reflect what is seen in you.

- Insist that your children save part of their allowance.

- Take them to restaurants that require waiting; do not always take them to fast food establishments.

- Play games that require taking turns.

Teach children selflessness. Children are naturally self centered. They need to be taught to care for others as well as caring for themselves. By teaching them this principle, they are more apt to be sensitive to the needs of others.

The more children think about themselves, the unhappier they will be. If they spend all the time thinking about what they want or what they do not have, they will never be satisfied with their lives. It is only when children can focus on others that they learn a sense of worthiness.

Below are some principles that you can use in teaching your child selflessness:

- Avoid bringing the child something back every time you go to the store.

- Have the child do something for someone else.

- Do something for others at Christmas time.

- Give presents on their birthday.

- Do something once a week for someone else.

- Help the elderly in the neighborhood.

Teach children good decision-making skills. By teaching children the six steps to decision making, you will give them the skills necessary to solve the simplest to the most complex of problems.

STEP 1: Define the problem. Before you can begin to solve the problem, you need to be clear on what the problem is? Often people fail to reach a satisfactory solution because they do not fully understand the problem.

You can help your children get a clear understanding of the problem. That does not mean that you tell them what it is, it means that you help them, through questions, to define the problem.

Remember, if you always solve their problems for them, they will never learn how to solve them on their own. If you teach them how, they will be more independent and responsible. Like the saying goes, "Give a man a fish and he will eat for a day. Teach him how to fish and he will eat for a lifetime."

STEP 2: List all possible solutions. When children are faced with a problem, they frequently reach roadblocks. You can be a tremendous help in generating several alternative solutions. This is what is called "Brainstorming." As you and your child "Brainstorm," it is important to remember these points:

- All ideas should be considered.

- Parent or the child do not criticize ideas.

- You need at least two ideas so that you will be able to make a choice.

- The length of the list of alternatives is not restricted.

STEP 3: List the positive and negative for each solution. The objective of the decision-making process is to make a decision that will leave children feeling good about themselves and about the choice. Examining consequences of each alternative gives them a better chance of achieving this goal and lessens the possibility of a poor decision.

STEP 4: Choose. Make a decision. Now as children are ready to make a decision, the following guidelines maybe helpful:

- The decision should help them feel better.

- The decision should not hurt others.

- The decision should help them grow.

STEP 5: Act. Do it.

STEP 6: Evaluate. Did it work? If you made a decision that did not work, try to figure out why it did not work. Go back to your list of alternatives, choose another one and repeat the process. You may also want to add new suggestions.

Teach children to be observers. Children need to watch the actions of others to determine what is socially and morally acceptable and unacceptable. You cannot be with your child twenty-four hours a day, but you can point things out to them when you are with them. They will follow your lead and begin to search for clues in the environment when you are not around.

Teach children to be discerners. Discernment is the ability to evaluate a situation or person and decide if the person or the situation meet your standards and expectations.

This does not happen without some teaching and instruction. In order to make sound judgments, children must have a solid base from which to operate.

Base #1—Sound Moral and Socially Acceptable Principles

Base #2—Good Observer

Base #3—Good Listener

Base #4—Good Decision-Making Skills

Because children do not automatically know what is acceptable and what is not, it is therefore paramount that you teach them right from wrong and principles to apply to situations when the answers are not clear cut. They need to know, for example:

- Do unto others as you would have others do unto you.

- If you feel that it is not right; it probably isn't.

- Honesty.

Teach children to be good listeners. Allen was telling Abigail about a bird flying around and finally landing on her roof. She told him the color of the bird was blue and grey. Abigail responded, "That's terrible." "Why," said Allen. A bird should not have a collar on."

Abigail responded as she did because she was not listening. Teach your children to be good listeners.

Teach children helpful and constructive ways of handling feelings. Children believe that feelings get them into trouble. They must be made to understand that it is not the feelings, but what they do or how they handle those feelings that cause problems.

The following may be helpful when teaching children this principle:

- Everyone has feelings.

- Feelings are not good or bad.

- Some feelings are warm and comfortable and some are cold and uncomfortable.

- Feelings should be handled in a way that does not hurt you or anyone else.

- Feelings do not get you into trouble; it is what you do with those feelings.

- It is important to let someone know how you feel.

- Feelings, comfortable or uncomfortable, only can be dealt with effectively when they are identified, acknowledged, and the source is determined. The worst thing anyone can do is to deny the existence of feelings.

Set rules and limits. Children should have a very clear understanding of what your expectations are. Rules and limits should be communicated thoroughly and then consistently enforced.

Do not take what you have already given. Once responsibilities are given to children, let them keep them. This will build confidence in their ability to handle more complex tasks in the future.

Provide rewards for responsible behavior. Some of these rewards should not be promised in advance but given spontaneously.

If children are acting in responsible ways in the absence of a promised reward, you know they are doing it for other reasons, not just for a prize.

Think before acting. Children must learn the importance of thinking before they act. Often when children fail to do this, they make very serious and avoidable mistakes.

I am sure that there are other ways of teaching children responsibility. You should seek to add to this list as your knowledge increase. Just remember, teaching responsibility is not a quick fix program or project—it's a way of life!

Educational Media Corporation®

ATTITUDE + DECISIONS + OWNERSHIP + CONSEQUENCES

Clues to Responsible Behavior

There are many behaviors that will help you to determine if a person is responsible. However, the basis of all of these is found in the definition of responsibility. Remember, responsibility was defined as Attitude (I believe that attitude needs to be clean. An attitude that is without malice, deceit, ill will and selfishness) + Decisions + Ownership + Consequences.

The list below was complied from this definition and the fifteen ways to teach responsibility. To be a responsible person, all four components (Attitude + Decision + Ownership + Consequences) must be present in the behavior.

If one or more of these components are missing, the result is "Fractured Responsibility." Like a broken leg, if one part does not function properly, the whole leg suffers. The person limps and is hindered from doing certain things until that leg completely heals. If the leg never heals, that individual would be limited by that condition.

So it is with Fractured Responsibility. Unless all the components are present and operating, being a responsible person is hindered because one of the following is missing: Attitude, Decisions, Ownership, (Willingness to own up to decisions—good or bad) or willingness to accept Consequences.

Just like it is difficult for a person to move from one place to another with a broken leg, Fractured Responsibility prevents us from being age appropriately responsible. A person may get older but is stuck on an inappropriate responsibility level because somewhere one of the components was left out.

As you read this list, keep in mind that a period of observation is necessary before a determination can be made as to the level of responsibility exhibited by an individual. If after careful examination you find Fractured Responsibility, please refer to the fifteen ways of teaching responsibility for assistance.

- Makes decisions that do not purposefully hurt self and others.
- Is considerate of others and their property.
- Is not unduly influenced by others.
- Is honest.
- Exhibits expected and accepted behaviors.
- Owns up to what one does without making excuses, blaming, justifying, or denying.
- Accepts consequences without anger or excessive arguing.
- Is willing to discuss inappropriate behaviors and alternative ways of handling the next problem without anger or guilt.
- Exercise patience and self control—age appropriate.
- Makes a decision to do what is right as opposed to what is popular.

- Is able to listen to another without interrupting.

- Consistently obeys rules and operates within established limits.

- Performs chores and other duties without being reminded.

- Completes tasks.

- Is able to be involved in age appropriate play without unwarranted supervision or undue attention for a period of time.

- Is truthful.

- Understands and can explain decisions.

- Promises are honored.

- Respects and likes self.

Note to Parents:

The principles that your children learn will be evident in their lives as adults. Your grandchildren will learn the same principles and in all likelihood embrace some of them as their own. I hope this book provided some assistance in helping you clarify the principles you endorse and seek to instill in your children. I trust that you also have additional tools as you work to structure discipline, raise your child's self-esteem, encourage cooperation, provide encouragement, and cultivate responsibility in your children.

Bibliography

Clemes, H., & Bean, R. (1990) *How to discipline children without feeling guilty.* Los Angeles: Price Stern Sloan.

Clemes, H., & Bean, R. (1990) *How to teach children responsibility.* Los Angeles: Price Stern Sloan.

Curwin, R.L., & Mendler, A.N. (1988). *Discipline with dignity.* Alexandria, VA: Association for Supervision and Curriculum Development.

Dobson, J., & Bauer, G.L. (1990). *Children at risk.* Dallas, TX: Word Publishing.

Dreikurs, R. (1987) *Children the challenge.* New York: Plume.

Popkin, M.H. (1983). *Active parenting.* Atlanta, GA: Active Parenting.

Rosemond, J.K. (1981). *Parent power.* Charlotte, NC: The East Woods Press.

Educational Media Corporation®